W9-CPH-225

Child Custody Issues

Child Custody Issues

David L. Hudson Jr.

SERIES EDITOR
Alan Marzilli, M.A., J.D.

CHELSEA HOUSE
An Infobase Learning Company

Child Custody Issues

Chelsea House
An imprint of Infobase Learning
132 West 31st Street
New York, NY 10001

Library of Congress Cataloging-in-Publication Data
Hudson, David L., 1969–
    Child custody issues / by David L. Hudson Jr.
    p. cm. — (Point/counterpoint)
    Includes bibliographical references and index.
    ISBN 978-1-60413-689-0 (hardcover)
    1. Custody of children—United States—Juvenile literature. I. Title.
    KF547.H83 2011
    346.7301'73—dc22
                                    2011001007

Chelsea House books are available at special discounts when purchased in bulk quantities for businesses, associations, institutions, or sales promotions. Please call our Special Sales Department in New York at (212) 967-8800 or (800) 322-8755.

You can find Chelsea House on the World Wide Web at
http://www.infobaselearning.com.

Text design by Keith Trego
Cover design by Alicia Post
Composition by EJB Publishing Services
Cover printed by Yurchak Printing, Landisville, Penn.
Book printed and bound by Yurchak Printing, Landisville, Penn.
Date printed: November 2011
Printed in the United States of America

This book is printed on acid-free paper.

All links and Web addresses were checked and verified to be correct at the time of publication. Because of the dynamic nature of the Web, some addresses and links may have changed since publication and may no longer be valid.

FOREWORD

Alan Marzilli, M.A., J.D.
Washington, D.C.

The POINT/COUNTERPOINT series offers the reader a greater understanding of some of the most controversial issues in contemporary American society—issues such as capital punishment, immigration, gay rights, and gun control. We have looked for the most contemporary issues and have included topics—such as the controversies surrounding "blogging"—that we could not have imagined when the series began.

In each volume, the author has selected an issue of particular importance and set out some of the key arguments on both sides of the issue. Why study both sides of the debate? Maybe you have yet to make up your mind on an issue, and the arguments presented in the book will help you to form an opinion. More likely, however, you will already have an opinion on many of the issues covered by the series. There is always the chance that you will change your opinion after reading the arguments for the other side. But even if you are firmly committed to an issue—for example, school prayer or animal rights—reading both sides of the argument will help you to become a more effective advocate for your cause. By gaining an understanding of opposing arguments, you can develop answers to those arguments.

Perhaps more importantly, listening to the other side sometimes helps you see your opponent's arguments in a more human way. For example, Sister Helen Prejean, one of the nation's most visible opponents of capital punishment, has been deeply affected by her interactions with the families of murder victims. By seeing the families' grief and pain, she understands much better why people support the death penalty, and she is able to carry out her advocacy with a greater sensitivity to the needs and beliefs of death penalty supporters.

The books in the series include numerous features that help the reader to gain a greater understanding of the issues. Real-life examples illustrate the human side of the issues. Each chapter also includes excerpts from relevant laws, court cases, and other material, which provide a better foundation for understanding the arguments. The volumes contain citations to relevant sources of law and information, and an appendix guides the reader through the basics of legal research, both on the Internet and in the library. Today, through free Web sites, it is easy to access legal documents, and these books might give you ideas for your own research.

Studying the issues covered by the POINT/COUNTERPOINT series is more than an academic activity. The issues described in the books affect all of us as citizens. They are the issues that today's leaders debate and tomorrow's leaders will decide. While all of the issues covered in the POINT/COUNTERPOINT series are controversial today, and will remain so for the foreseeable future, it is entirely possible that the reader might one day play a central role in resolving the debate. Today it might seem that some debates—such as capital punishment and abortion—will never be resolved.

However, our nation's history is full of debates that seemed as though they never would be resolved, and many of the issues are now well settled—at least on the surface. In the nineteenth century, abolitionists met with widespread resistance to their efforts to end slavery. Ultimately, the controversy threatened the union, leading to the Civil War between the northern and southern states. Today, while a public debate over the merits of slavery would be unthinkable, racism persists in many aspects of society.

Similarly, today nobody questions women's right to vote. Yet at the beginning of the twentieth century, suffragists fought public battles for women's voting rights, and it was not until the passage of the Nineteenth Amendment in 1920 that the legal right of women to vote was established nationwide.

What makes an issue controversial? Often, controversies arise when most people agree that there is a problem but disagree about the best way to solve it. There is little argument that poverty is a major problem in the United States, especially in inner cities and rural areas. Yet, people disagree vehemently about the best way to address the problem. To some, the answer is social programs, such as welfare, food stamps, and public housing. However, many argue that such subsidies encourage dependence on government benefits while unfairly penalizing those who work and pay taxes, and that the real solution is to require people to support themselves.

American society is in a constant state of change, and sometimes modern practices clash with what many consider to be "traditional values," which are often rooted in conservative political views or religious beliefs. Many blame high crime rates, and problems such as poverty, illiteracy, and drug use on the breakdown of the traditional family structure of a married mother and father raising their children. Since the "sexual revolution" of the 1960s and 1970s, sparked in part by the widespread availability of the birth control pill, marriage rates have declined, and the number of children born outside of marriage has increased. The sexual revolution led to controversies over birth control, sex education, and other issues, most prominently abortion. Similarly, the gay rights movement has been challenged as a threat to traditional values. While many gay men and lesbians want to have the same right to marry and raise families as heterosexuals, many politicians and others have challenged gay marriage and adoption as a threat to American society.

Sometimes, new technology raises issues that we have never faced before, and society disagrees about the best solution. Are people free to swap music online, or does this violate the copyright laws that protect songwriters and musicians' ownership of the music that they create? Should scientists use "genetic engineering" to create new crops that are resistant to disease and pests and produce more food, or is it too risky to use a laboratory to create plants that nature never intended? Modern medicine has continued to increase the average lifespan—which is now 77 years, up from under 50 years at the beginning of the twentieth century—but many people are now choosing to die in comfort rather than living with painful ailments in their later years. For doctors, this presents an ethical dilemma: should they allow their patients to die? Should they assist patients in ending their own lives painlessly?

Perhaps the most controversial issues are those that implicate a Constitutional right. The Bill of Rights—the first 10 Amendments to the U.S. Constitution—spells out some of the most fundamental rights that distinguish our democracy from other nations with fewer freedoms. However, the sparsely worded document is open to interpretation, with each side saying that the Constitution is on their side. The Bill of Rights was meant to protect individual liberties; however, the needs of some individuals clash with society's needs. Thus, the Constitution often serves as a battleground between individuals and government officials seeking to protect society in some way. The First Amendment's guarantee of "freedom of speech" leads to some very difficult questions. Some forms of expression—such as burning an American flag—lead to public outrage, but are protected by the First Amendment. Other types of expression that most people find objectionable—such as child pornography—are not protected by the Constitution. The question is not only where to draw the line, but whether drawing lines around constitutional rights threatens our liberty.

The Bill of Rights raises many other questions about individual rights and societal "good." Is a prayer before a high school football game an "establishment of religion" prohibited by the First Amendment? Does the Second Amendment's promise of "the right to bear arms" include concealed handguns? Does stopping and frisking someone standing on a known drug corner constitute "unreasonable search and seizure" in violation of the Fourth Amendment? Although the U.S. Supreme Court has the ultimate authority in interpreting the U.S. Constitution, its answers do not always satisfy the public. When a group of nine people—sometimes by a five-to-four vote—makes a decision that affects hundreds of millions of others, public outcry can be expected. For example, the Supreme Court's 1973 ruling in *Roe v. Wade* that abortion is protected by the Constitution did little to quell the debate over abortion.

Whatever the root of the controversy, the books in the POINT/ COUNTERPOINT series seek to explain to the reader the origins of the debate, the current state of the law, and the arguments on either side of the debate. Our hope in creating this series is that readers will be better informed about the issues facing not only our politicians, but all of our nation's citizens, and become more actively involved in resolving these debates, as voters, concerned citizens, journalists, or maybe even elected officials.

This issue covered in this volume provides an excellent example of how laws and policies often must change in order to reflect changes in society at large. As divorce and familial dislocation have become more common in the United States, the need for the law to be flexible in child custody disputes has been highlighted. Laws surrounding the custody of children when their two parents do not live together have shifted in recent decades, but like most laws designed to settle disputes between competing interests, they often leave one or more parties unhappy with the results. With the decline of manufacturing jobs, general population shifts southward and westward, and the globalization of industries, our society has become more mobile. Parents often move from state to state for various reasons, and when custody is shared with another parent, such moves generate controversy. Of particular interest is how states view phone, e-mail, or video chat as a substitute for in-person contact. Social views of dating and marriage across racial and ethnic lines have also changed, yet race and ethnicity still generate controversy when determining custody of children. Laws vary from state to state and are subject to frequent changes, and this book examines some of the debates that drive these changes.

An Overview of Child Custody

Divorce represents one of the toughest and emotionally grueling experiences a person may experience in life. The dissolution of a marital union also can be a very complex legal matter. The parties to the former marriage have to divide up property, which includes both assets and debts. They have to determine whether one party will have to provide financial support, called alimony, to the other party and for how long. They have to determine who receives the family home, the vehicles, and other assets, as well as settle any other outstanding financial issues.

Divorce becomes even more complicated and emotionally charged if there are children involved. In that case, the courts often have to determine who receives primary custody of the children. These are gut-wrenching cases that can leave lasting impacts on both parents and adults. As attorney Susan W. Savard writes: "High-conflict family law litigation is extremely detrimental not only to the parents but also to the children involved as well."[1]

Child custody and visitation represents a major area of family law. Courts are called upon to make such determinations not only in the case of divorce, but also in cases in which the parents were never married or even maintained a long-term relationship. There are two basic types of child custody: sole custody and joint custody. In sole custody, one parent has legal custody of the child and makes the major life decisions for the child. In joint custody, the parents share legal custody of the child, though one parent is normally considered the primary custodial parent or the parent with whom the child lives most of the time.[2]

States often distinguish between joint *legal* custody and joint *physical* custody. California law, for example, defines joint legal custody as "both parents shall share the right and the responsibility to make the decisions relating to the health, education, and welfare of a child."[3] California law classifies joint physical custody as "each of the parents [having] significant periods of physical custody. Joint physical custody shall be shared by the parents in such a way so as to assure a child of frequent and continuing contact with both parents."[4] It defines sole legal custody as "one parent shall have the right and the responsibility to make the decisions relating to the health, education, and welfare of a child."[5] And it classifies sole physical custody as "a child shall reside with and be under the supervision of one parent, subject to the power of the court to order visitation."[6]

States use different terminology for custody—some states use the terms partial custody, legal custody, or shared custody. Whichever parent does not receive primary custody receives so-called visitation rights. In many jurisdictions, a common visitation plan is that the noncustodial parent has the child every other weekend and for an extended period of time over the summer months. Parents work out the custody arrangement during the divorce decree—the formal, legal document that outlines the divorce and its impact upon the family.

Oftentimes, however, the two parties battle over custody and visitation issues for years. One parent may argue, for example, that the other is not providing sufficient visitation rights. Or one parent may claim that the other parent has kept the kids too long on a visitation stay. In an even more charged atmosphere, a parent may file for a change of custody. The parent doing the filing is typically the noncustodial parent, who believes he or she should become the primary custodial parent instead of the other parent. In most states, the noncustodial parent must show a "material change in circumstances" for a court to change the basic custody arrangement.

Material changes of circumstances could include an arrest for domestic violence, any incidence of child abuse, excessive moving to different locations, a sharp reduction in a child's grades, or a glaring lack of adult supervision of the child in the custodial home. Another example of a material change of circumstances could be that one parent consistently refuses to allow the noncustodial parent to exercise his or her visitation rights according to a court-ordered parenting plan in the divorce decree.[7]

This book examines three controversial and contentious areas of child custody law. The first issue involves the "best interests of the child standard," which is the leading litmus test used to determine custody and change of custody matters. In most states, there is a law that sets forth numerous factors for the court to consider "the best interests of the child." These often include such things as the reasonable preference of the child, the physical and mental stability of the parents, the emotional bonds between the child and the parents, and whether a parent has committed an act of domestic violence. In the Point chapter, the best interests standard is presented as a flexible, helpful standard that allows judges to render decisions on a case-by-case basis. In the Counterpoint chapter, the argument advanced establishes that the standard leads to inconsistent results, elevates parental interests over the children's interests, and performs poorly.

The next issue concerns a particularly thorny area of child custody: parental relocation. When the custodial parent relocates with the child to another part of the state or country, this relocation often negatively impacts the visitation rights of the

THE LETTER OF THE LAW

Examples of Definitions of Legal Custody from the Alabama and Tennessee State Legislatures

Alabama Child Custody Guidelines

For the purposes of this article the following words shall have the following meanings:

(1) **Joint custody.** Joint legal custody and joint physical custody.

(2) **Joint legal custody.** Both parents have equal rights and responsibilities for major decisions concerning the child, including, but not limited to, the education of the child, health care, and religious training. The court may designate one parent to have sole power to make certain decisions while both parents retain equal rights and responsibilities for other decisions.

(3) **Joint physical custody.** Physical custody is shared by the parents in a way that assures the child frequent and substantial contact with each parent. Joint physical custody does not necessarily mean physical custody of equal durations of time.

(4) **Sole legal custody.** One parent has sole rights and responsibilities to make major decisions concerning the child, including, but not limited to, the education of the child, health care, and religious training.

(5) **Sole physical custody.** One parent has sole physical custody and the other parent has rights of visitation except as otherwise provided by the court.*

Tennessee State Law on "Material Change of Circumstances" in Custody Cases

(B) If the issue before the court is a modification of the court's prior decree pertaining to custody, the petitioner must prove by a preponderance of the evidence a material change in circumstance. A material change of

noncustodial parent. The Point chapter contends that in this global economy, custodial parents should have greater leeway in relocations in order to improve the quality of life for their children. It argues that the basic bond that needs the law's protection

circumstance does not require a showing of a substantial risk of harm to the child. A material change of circumstance may include, but is not limited to, failures to adhere to the parenting plan or an order of custody and visitation or circumstances that make the parenting plan no longer in the best interest of the child.

(i) In each contested case, the court shall make such a finding as to the reason and the facts that constitute the basis for the custody determination.

(ii) Nothing contained within the provisions of this subdivision (a)(2) shall interfere with the requirement that parties to an action for legal separation, annulment, absolute divorce or separate maintenance incorporate a parenting plan into the final decree or decree modifying an existing custody order.

(iii) Nothing in this subsection (a) shall imply a mandatory modification to the child support order.

(C) If the issue before the court is a modification of the court's prior decree pertaining to a residential parenting schedule, then the petitioner must prove by a preponderance of the evidence a material change of circumstance affecting the child's best interest. A material change of circumstance does not require a showing of a substantial risk of harm to the child. A material change of circumstance for purposes of modification of a residential parenting schedule may include, but is not limited to, significant changes in the needs of the child over time, which may include changes relating to age; significant changes in the parent's living or working condition that significantly affect parenting; failure to adhere to the parenting plan; or other circumstances making a change in the residential parenting time in the best interest of the child.**

* Alabama Code, Section 30-3-151.
** T.C.A. 36-6-101.

Though they have declined somewhat in recent years, divorce rates in the United States are the highest in the world. Because people divorce for a variety of reasons, courts typically take into consideration the "best interests of the child" in order to determine custody issues.

is the child's bond with the primary caregiver. The Counterpoint chapter answers that argument by noting how relocation often harms children by uprooting them from their established routine. It argues that the burden should be placed on the moving custodial parent and that moving children often is harmful to their emotional well-being.

The final issue examined on both sides concerns the issue of race—something that is still a matter of considerable debate in American society. The Point chapter argues that race should never be a factor in custody decisions, that courts should decide child custody cases in a completely color-blind manner. The chapter advances the argument that considering race in child custody matters furthers discrimination and, moreover, violates the Equal Protection Clause of the Fourteenth Amendment. The Counterpoint chapter answers this by noting that race and ethnicity may be important factors in a child custody decision, as long as it is not the sole factor. The chapter contends that sometimes, particularly in an interracial marriage, one parent may be able to help the child deal with racial identity better than the other parent.

The Best Interests Standard Works in Child Custody Disputes

A bitter divorce ends the 20-year marriage of a couple who have three underage children. Both parents argue over custody of the children. At one time, the court would have expressed a stark preference for either the mother or the father. A generation ago, for example, gender preferences meant that the mother would receive primary custody, and the father only visiting rights. He would also likely have to pay child support. Today, however, under existing state laws, the judge has the ability to sift through many different factors to make the best decision for all parties involved. The judge may consider the preferences of the children, the mental and physical health of both parents, the emotional bonds between the children and the respective parents, and the moral fitness of both parents.

Our modern perspective on child custody, which considers the best interests of the children involved, is preferable to the way in which these matters were settled years ago. The law should give judges the needed flexibility to make the best decision possible under trying circumstances. Every case is different, just as every human being is different. Clearly, the "best interests of the child" standard is the best standard available to decide admittedly very difficult questions.

Favoring one gender over another does not work.

The law used to not care about the wishes of the child. Instead, legal systems simply assumed that the child was better off with the father or the mother. In the English common-law system of the 1600s, the concept of *patria potestas*, or paternal power, meant that fathers controlled the family. What a father said went, no questions asked. This also meant that fathers had final say on all matters related to children, including custody. Professor Steven Peskind relates that "the history of Western culture reflected children as the property of their father, which resulted in their total control by that father."[1]

In the United States, during the early part of the twentieth century, many state laws shifted dramatically to a system in which the mother became the naturally preferred parent. Part of this was due to the evolving role of women in American society. Women achieved the right to vote with the ratification of the Nineteenth Amendment in 1920 and began to achieve greater social inclusion. Society also began to appreciate and recognize the power of "maternal instincts" as essential to improving the lives of children.[2] This preference became known as the so-called "tender years doctrine."

Gradually over time, the current gender-neutral best interests standard took precedence over the material preference inherent in the tender years doctrine. The shattering of traditional norms of women as family caretakers in the 1960s and 1970s created a climate necessary for this change. As women entered the workforce in larger numbers and became more involved in maintaining their own finances, the courts did not

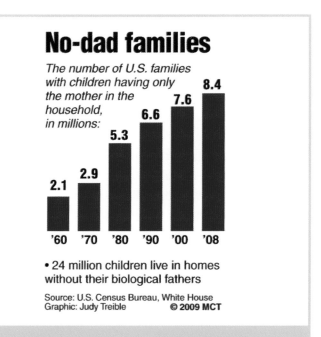

No-dad families

The number of U.S. families with children having only the mother in the household, in millions:

2.1   2.9   5.3   6.6   7.6   8.4

'60   '70   '80   '90   '00   '08

• 24 million children live in homes without their biological fathers

Source: U.S. Census Bureau, White House
Graphic: Judy Treible   © 2009 MCT

This chart from 2009 shows the growth of the number of families with children who have only their mothers in the household. Because such families have become far more common since 1960, child custody issues have had to adapt to changing demographics and circumstances.

see them as automatically the best parents to have primary custody of their children. Still, some courts still considered the need for maternal love as a key factor in child custody cases. For example, the Kansas Supreme Court ruled in 1981 that the tender years doctrine could serve as a tiebreaker in a close custody case. In *Grubbs v. Grubbs* (1981), the Kansas high court wrote that "the age of the child and need for maternal care are merely factors to be considered in reaching that ultimate conclusion."[3] The Tennessee Court of Appeals reached a similar conclusion in *Bah v. Bah* (1983) when it determined that "the so-called 'tender years' doctrine is a factor—but only one factor—to be considered in the overall determination of what is in the best interests of the child."[4]

"The maternal presumption continued until the mid-1970s and several standards were created to supplement the tender years doctrine," writes legal commentator Shannon Dean Sexton. "These standards maintained a maternal presumption: unless the mother was proven unfit, or the father could prove he deserved custody by 'compelling evidence,' the mother was awarded custody."[5]

Other proposed standards based on general assumptions regarding fathers and mothers are not any better. The interests of the child should trump the interests of the parents. Some have proposed deferring to the parents and allowing parents to make key decisions regarding child custody. This is a bad idea, as children are not property but living human beings who should not be bartered.

The best interests standard considers many helpful factors.

The best interests standard is useful because it contains so many helpful factors that courts should consider in deciding custody cases. A common question in a custody proceeding is which parent has served as the primary caregiver and nurturer of the child.[6] Typically, a parent who has been the primary caregiver knows what is best for the child under a variety of circumstances, especially if the child is very young. This factor can be particularly important in situations in which a biological parent who has had little to no involvement suddenly decides to become involved in a child's life.

Many state standards in determining best interests of the child also consider the mental and physical health of each parent. This factor is helpful because it allows courts to consider whether a parent has emotional problems that could negatively impact the parent-child relationship. If a parent has severe physical impairments, this could be important in determining the care of a child, as he or she might be incapable of keeping up with the demands of parenthood.

Another common factor used in determining best interests is whether one of the parents has committed domestic violence.[7] Indiana law looks at "evidence of a pattern of domestic or family violence by either parent."[8] It is vitally important for courts to consider whether a parent has perpetrated acts of violence, as courts wish to avoid placing children with violent people. Moreover, many states consider the moral fitness of each parent. If a parent engages in criminal activity of any kind, such as possessing or selling illegal drugs, a court would be unlikely to place a young child in such a harmful environment.

What other factors do courts consider? Many states allow judges to evaluate the "reasonable preference" of the child, if the court determines the child is old enough to make that determination.[9] Courts should emphasize this factor if they are going to pay credence to the best interests of the child.

Best interests laws provide a needed degree of flexibility.

Sometimes a parent who provides a greater income is not the better parent to rear children on a day-to-day basis. An otherwise loving parent may have a serious temper problem, which can increase the possibility of violence. Sometimes, a mother or father may be a good parent but has an abusive boyfriend or girlfriend who could be a threat to the child's well-being. Other times, a child simply has a much better rapport with one parent or another. Occasionally, one parent may have certain mental or physical health problems that could negatively impact the rearing of the child. Finally, a parent may engage in questionable conduct, or even illegal activity, that threatens the well-being of the family unit.

There is no one factor that judges employ in order to make this most vital decision. The future of a child's life and well-being is literally at stake at such moments; therefore courts

THE LETTER OF THE LAW

Michigan's Definition of "Best Interests"

§ 722.23. "Best interests of the child" defined.

As used in this act, "best interests of the child" means the sum total of the following factors to be considered, evaluated, and determined by the court:

(a) The love, affection, and other emotional ties existing between the parties involved and the child.

(b) The capacity and disposition of the parties involved to give the child love, affection, and guidance and to continue the education and raising of the child in his or her religion or creed, if any.

(c) The capacity and disposition of the parties involved to provide the child with food, clothing, medical care or other remedial care recognized and permitted under the laws of this state in place of medical care, and other material needs.

(d) The length of time the child has lived in a stable, satisfactory environment, and the desirability of maintaining continuity.

(e) The permanence, as a family unit, of the existing or proposed custodial home or homes.

(f) The moral fitness of the parties involved.

(g) The mental and physical health of the parties involved.

(h) The home, school, and community record of the child.

(i) The reasonable preference of the child, if the court considers the child to be of sufficient age to express preference.

(j) The willingness and ability of each of the parties to facilitate and encourage a close and continuing parent-child relationship between the child and the other parent or the child and the parents.

(k) Domestic violence, regardless of whether the violence was directed against or witnessed by the child.

(l) Any other factor considered by the court to be relevant to a particular child custody dispute.

Source: MCLS § 722.23.

must use a multitude of factors in rendering their decisions. For these reasons, it is clear that using the best interests standard is not only practical, but also necessary, in child custody cases. As Professor Peskind writes: "The best interest standard must necessarily be open ended because each individual child and family situation is unique."[10]

THE LETTER OF THE LAW

North Dakota Law on Determining "Best Interests"

1. For the purpose of parental rights and responsibilities, the best interests and welfare of the child is determined by the court's consideration and evaluation of all factors affecting the best interests and welfare of the child. These factors include all of the following when applicable:

   a. The love, affection, and other emotional ties existing between the parents and child and the ability of each parent to provide the child with nurture, love, affection, and guidance.

   b. The ability of each parent to assure that the child receives adequate food, clothing, shelter, medical care, and a safe environment.

   c. The child's developmental needs and the ability of each parent to meet those needs, both in the present and in the future.

   d. The sufficiency and stability of each parent's home environment, the impact of extended family, the length of time the child has lived in each parent's home, and the desirability of maintaining continuity in the child's home and community.

   e. The willingness and ability of each parent to facilitate and encourage a close and continuing relationship between the other parent and the child.

   f. The moral fitness of the parents, as that fitness impacts the child.

   g. The mental and physical health of the parents, as that health impacts the child.

   h. The home, school, and community record of the child and the potential effect of any change.

The best interests standard is the best available option.

Because of the many factors involved in rendering a verdict, critics, who see it as too flexible, attack the best interest standard. Yet, there is no better option. Every case needs to be evaluated carefully, through various means, because every child is vitally

---

i. If the court finds by clear and convincing evidence that a child is of sufficient maturity to make a sound judgment, the court may give substantial weight to the preference of the mature child. The court also shall give due consideration to other factors that may have affected the child's preference, including whether the child's preference was based on undesirable or improper influences.

j. Evidence of domestic violence. In determining parental rights and responsibilities, the court shall consider evidence of domestic violence. If the court finds credible evidence that domestic violence has occurred, and there exists one incident of domestic violence which resulted in serious bodily injury or involved the use of a dangerous weapon or there exists a pattern of domestic violence within a reasonable time proximate to the proceeding, this combination creates a rebuttable presumption that a parent who has perpetrated domestic violence may not be awarded residential responsibility for the child. This presumption may be overcome only by clear and convincing evidence that the best interests of the child require that parent have residential responsibility. . . .

k. The interaction and interrelationship, or the potential for interaction and interrelationship, of the child with any person who resides in, is present, or frequents the household of a parent and who may significantly affect the child's best interests. The court shall consider that person's history of inflicting, or tendency to inflict, physical harm, bodily injury, assault, or the fear of physical harm, bodily injury, or assault, on other persons.

l. The making of false allegations not made in good faith, by one parent against the other. . . . Any other factors considered by the court to be relevant to a particular parental rights and responsibilities dispute. . . .

Source: North Dakota Century Code Ann. 14-09-06.2.

important. "The best interests of the child doctrine is at once the most heralded, derided and relied upon standard in family law today," Professor Lynne Marie Kohm writes. "It is heralded because it espouses the best and highest standard; it is derided because it is necessarily subjective; and it is relied upon because there is nothing better."[11]

Some criticize the standard because it can lead to different results (depending on the case) and also because it often requires a judge to weigh numerous factors. That said, the best interests standard has proven to be the most reliable way to provide the finest outcome for the children involved in each custody case. Professor Steven N. Peskind notes that even though the standard has problems, "there simply is no better way to resolve contested issues affecting children."[12] He explains that "instead of trying to avoid contested litigation, the courts need to embrace its inevitability" and that "courts must develop a means of accommodating an indeterminate best interest standard, and work to refine its implementation through concrete means designed to resolve custody disputes as efficiently and fairly as possible."[13] Rather than tear down the system, critics should work to make sure that the courts are considering the proper factors on a case-by-case basis and that attorneys are educated in how to best present child custody cases.

Summary

The best interests standard is the gold-standard option available for courts to deal with thorny child custody issues. It provides a wide range of factors for courts to consider in determining what really is best for children under specific circumstances. Often, it is important to know the preferences of a child, the emotional bonds between parent and child, the moral fitness of the parents, the emotional and physical health of the parents, the absence of domestic violence, and many other factors.

The best interests standard is a vast improvement over every other standard that has been previously employed. Stark gender preferences for either the mother or father are simply unfair. Children are not property, so bartering children in a way similar to a prenuptial agreement that deals with questions of alimony and property is not only unseemly but also morally wrong. The interests of the children should predominate and the standard should be flexible. There is no better standard available. Rather than try to tear down the best interests standard as it exists, interested observers and advocates should work to better refine the standard.

The Best Interests Standard Is Too Subjective

In Case A, a mother and father with an underage male child divorce. The mother had been the primary caregiver of the child, while the father had provided the bulk of the financial resources. Both parents are active in the child's life and the child has solid emotional bonds with each. The boy, who is 12 years old, has expressed a desire to live with his father. Neither party has committed an act of domestic violence. The trial court rules that because the mother is the primary caregiver, the child should reside with her.

In Case B, a mother and father with a minor female child divorce. The mother and father have both worked outside the home though the mother still served as the primary day-to-day caregiver. The parties' 13-year-old daughter expressed a desire to remain with her mother. Neither party had committed an act of domestic violence. The mother, however, had a bout with depression several years ago after the death of her parents, and the father had to attend an anger management class after an altercation at a local store years ago. The trial court rules that the father had greater emotional and physical stability and determined that the child should reside with the father as the primary custodial parent.

In Case C, a mother and father with two underage children divorce. The mother and father both work outside the home. The father has served as the primary caregiver, as his job provided a greater degree of flexibility. The parties' 12-year-old twins split in their preferences. One child expressed a desire to live with the mother, while the other prefers to live with the father. Both the mother and the father had no incidents of domestic violence, but the parties had a great deal of acrimony during the divorce.

(continues on page 32)

THE LETTER OF THE LAW

Many states have catchall categories written into their legal systems to help judges determine the best interests of children who are involved in custody cases. The following are some excerpts from relevant state statutes:

California: Cal. Fam. Code § 3011
"In making a determination of the best interest of the child in a proceeding described in Section 3021, the court shall, among any other factors it finds relevant..."

Michigan
"Any other factor considered by the court to be relevant to a particular child custody dispute."

Utah: Utah Code Ann. § 30-3-10.2(2)(j)
"...any other factors the court finds relevant."

Virginia: Va. Code Ann. § 20-124.3(10)
"Such other factors as the court deems necessary and proper to the determination."

THE LETTER OF THE LAW

Excerpts from Two States' Best Interests of the Child Standards

Indiana Code—Chapter 13. Custody Following Determination of Paternity

Factors of custody determination

31-14-13-2 Sec. 2.

The court shall determine custody in accordance with the best interests of the child. In determining the child's best interests, there is not a presumption favoring either parent. The court shall consider all relevant factors, including the following:

(1) The age and sex of the child.

(2) The wishes of the child's parents.

(3) The wishes of the child, with more consideration given to the child's wishes if the child is at least fourteen (14) years of age.

(4) The interaction and interrelationship of the child with:

(A) the child's parents;

(B) the child's siblings; and

(C) any other person who may significantly affect the child's best interest.

(5) The child's adjustment to home, school, and community.

(6) The mental and physical health of all individuals involved.

(7) Evidence of a pattern of domestic or family violence by either parent.

(8) Evidence that the child has been cared for by a de facto custodian, and if the evidence is sufficient, the court shall consider the factors described in section 2.5(b) [IC 31-14-13-2.5(b)] of this chapter.*

Tennessee Code Annotated

Title 36 Domestic Relations

Chapter 6 Child Custody and Visitation

Part 1—General Custody Provisions

36-6-106. Child custody.

(a) In a suit for annulment, divorce, separate maintenance, or in any other proceeding requiring the court to make a custody determination regarding a minor child, the determination shall be made on the basis of the best interest of the child. The court shall consider all relevant factors, including the following, where applicable:

(1) The love, affection and emotional ties existing between the parents or caregivers and the child;

(2) The disposition of the parents or caregivers to provide the child with food, clothing, medical care, education and other necessary care and the degree to which a parent or caregiver has been the primary caregiver;

(3) The importance of continuity in the child's life and the length of time the child has lived in a stable, satisfactory environment; provided, that, where there is a finding, under subdivision (a)(8), of child abuse, as defined in § 39-15-401 or § 39-15-402, or child sexual abuse, as defined in § 37-1-602, by one (1) parent, and that a nonperpetrating parent or caregiver has relocated in order to flee the perpetrating parent, that the relocation shall not weigh against an award of custody;

(4) The stability of the family unit of the parents or caregivers;

(5) The mental and physical health of the parents or caregivers;

(6) The home, school and community record of the child;

(7) (A) The reasonable preference of the child, if twelve (12) years of age or older;

(B) The court may hear the preference of a younger child on request. The preferences of older children should normally be given greater weight than those of younger children;

(8) Evidence of physical or emotional abuse to the child, to the other parent or to any other person; provided, that, where there are allegations that one (1) parent has committed child abuse, as defined in § 39-15-401 or § 39-15-402, or child sexual abuse, as defined in § 37-1-602, against a family member, the court shall consider all evidence relevant to the physical and emotional safety of the child, and determine, by a clear preponderance of the evidence, whether such abuse has occurred. The court shall include in its decision a written finding of all evidence, and all findings of facts connected to the evidence. In addition, the court shall, where appropriate, refer any issues of abuse to the juvenile court for further proceedings;

(continues)

THE LETTER OF THE LAW

(continued)

(9) The character and behavior of any other person who resides in or frequents the home of a parent or caregiver and the person's interactions with the child; and

(10) (A) Each parent or caregiver's past and potential for future performance of parenting responsibilities, including the willingness and ability of each of the parents and caregivers to facilitate and encourage a close and continuing parent-child relationship between the child and both of the child's parents, consistent with the best interest of the child.

   (B) Notwithstanding the provisions of any law to the contrary, the court has jurisdiction to make an initial custody determination regarding a minor child or may modify a prior order of child custody upon finding that the custodial parent has been convicted of or found civilly liable for the intentional and wrongful death of the child's other parent or legal guardian.**

* Indiana Code 31-14-13.
** T.C.A. 36-6-106.

(continued from page 29)
The trial court determines that the mother should have primary custody, believing that the father would not respect the visitation rights of the mother if he were the primary custodial parent.

These three cases demonstrate the problems that exist with the best interests standard. Litigants, attorneys, and others simply cannot predict with certainty how these cases will be decided.

There are too many variables in the best interests standard.

Supporters of the best interests standard tout the fact that it provides great flexibility and gives judges the opportunity to consider each custody dispute on a case-by-case basis. Unfortunately for the parties involved, the multitude of factors leads to often-unpredictable judgments. Furthermore, results can vary based on the state in which the case is heard, because state laws may modify the standard legal doctrine.

And the modifications themselves vary greatly. A few examples to reflect on: Indiana law allows that the age and sex of the child may be considered in determining which parent should have primary custody.[1] Oregon provides that there should be a preference for the primary caregiver of the child as long as that person is a fit parent.[2] Virginia considers the age of the parents as a relevant factor.[3] Delaware law considers relevant to the child custody determination whether a parent has any type of criminal conviction, including a guilty plea.[4] Arizona law looks at whether either party was convicted of filing a false criminal report of child abuse.[5] Montana determines whether a parent failed to pay birth-related costs of the child or failed to provide support for the child if able.[6] Georgia considers each parent's employment schedule and the flexibility in which they schedule their job hours.[7] Minnesota allows for the consideration of the child and parent's cultural backgrounds.[8] Nevada looks at whether a child will be able to maintain a relationship with any siblings.[9] Idaho law has a clause that provides: "The character and circumstances of all individuals involved."[10] Colorado has a factor that provides: "The ability of each party to place the needs of the child ahead of his or her own needs."[11]

The variations are not only bewildering, but can also be all-inclusive: Many states have a catchall category that allows judges to consider *any* factor they deem relevant. This is simply too much discretion. Most states list more than 10 factors when judges consider the best interests of children. When you list this many factors, courts are free to pick which factors they wish to emphasize.

The best interests standard leads to inconsistent results.

The best interests standard is too inconsistent and biased. Imagine, if you will, a criminal court case in which someone was on trial for theft or murder and the judge and jury were allowed to weigh an extraordinary number of variables (including their own prejudices) before coming to a verdict and sentencing. Would this be fair or provide a just ruling? In any legal setting, it is above all important to provide rulings that are consistent, fair, and balanced. Without an expectation of impartiality and a clear framework by which judgments are made, the parties involved in custody disputes have no expectation that a judge will provide them with justice. A leading treatise on family law declares that "such broad discretion [with the best interests standard] obviously carries the potential for subjective decisions that may be tainted by personal bias or lack of understanding of child development."[12] Law professor Lynne Marie Kohm explains that the application of the standard "has turned toward near pure judicial discretion in contemporary judging, causing litigators and advocates to have no rule of law to rely on."[13]

The standard should focus more on the preference of the children.

If there is to be a best interests standard, it should take into consideration what the children involved in a custody proceeding truly want. Their wants and needs are of paramount importance. To that end, the family law codes in many states should be changed to elevate the reasonable preference of children above all other considerations. In many states the law provides that the preference of a child may be considered if the child is more than 12 or 14 years of age. The law should not only consider the preferences of younger children, it should also make it a determinative or a major factor in any child custody decision. The legal system cannot claim to be acting in the best interests of children if it does not elevate the preference of the child to a higher place than it currently receives under the law. State legislatures should amend their child custody laws in a manner similar to the state of Georgia, which provides that a court should consider the preference of a child 14 years of age or older to be controlling unless the parent chosen is deemed unfit.[14]

Summary
The best interests standard—at least as currently implemented by the courts—contain too many discretionary factors, lead to inconsistent results, and fail to provide sufficient guidance to

---

THE LETTER OF THE LAW

Excerpt from Georgia's Law on Preference of Child as Controlling

(A) In all cases in which the child has reached the age of 14 years, the child shall have the right to select the parent with whom he or she desires to live. The child's selection shall be controlling, unless the parent so selected is determined not to be a fit and proper person to have the custody of the child.

(B) In all cases in which the child has reached the age of at least 11 but not 14 years, the court shall consider the desires, if any, and educational needs of the child in determining which parent shall have custody. The court shall have complete discretion in making this determination, and the child's desires are not controlling. The court shall further have broad discretion as to how the child's desires are to be considered, including through the report of a guardian *ad litem*. The best interest of the child standard shall be controlling.

(C) The desire of a child who has reached the age of 11 years but not 14 years shall not, in and of itself, constitute a material change of conditions or circumstances in any action seeking a modification or change in the custody of that child.

(D) The court may issue an order granting temporary custody to the selected parent for a trial period not to exceed six months regarding the custody of a child who has reached the age of at least 11 years where the judge hearing the case determines such a temporary order is appropriate.

Source: O.C.G.A. 19-9-1.

parents, attorneys, and judges. Many state laws provide for a litany of factors in making best interests determinations, which not only convolutes the process but also undermines the fairness of the legal system in providing the best results for all parties involved. Some states have even written laws that allow judges to consider any other factor they personally deem necessary or important. As a result, the best interests standard has turned many custody hearings into an almost capricious farce.

Though problems exist, there are some options available for reforming the legal system. One option is that the system could elevate the interests of children by giving their preference real determination in custody cases, rather than making it simply one factor among many. Another option would be to defer to the reasoned judgment of parents by having them make custodial arrangements even before they entered into marriage.

Laws Should Favor the Custodial Parent in Relocation Disputes

A mother serves as the primary custodial parent of her young son. Since the boy's birth, she has worked as his primary caretaker because the father did not want anything to do with the child. In fact, the father initially had refused to even acknowledge that the child was his. After a court order established his paternity and forced him to pay child support, the father then asserted his right to custody. Through the intervening years, the father has maintained intermittent contact with his child through visitation.

When the mother and father lived in the same town for some years, the father was able to assert his visitation rights whenever he wished. The mother, however, has received a new job offer in another state. This new job provides a significant pay raise and a way to provide more opportunities for the young child. Additionally, the mother's new significant other resides in this other state.

The father balks at the proposed move, even though it will benefit the child financially. He contends that such a move will deprive him of his constitutional rights to assert his custody. This phenomenon is not at all uncommon in the United States, as a noncustodial parent often contends that his or her visitation rights should trump the ability of the custodial parent to provide a better life for the child or children they share. The growing global economy increases the likelihood that the custodial parent may have job opportunities that are removed from the noncustodial parent.

Admittedly, these cases present tough problems for courts, as there are competing interests of the custodial and noncustodial parents to consider. The custodial parent sometimes needs to relocate to provide a better life for their child or children. Yet, as selfless a reason as that may seem, the noncustodial parent has a strong interest in maintaining a relationship with the child. As the Supreme Court of South Carolina explained in 2004 in the case of *Latimer v. Farmer*:

> Cases involving the relocation of a custodial parent with a minor child bring into direct conflict a custodial parent's freedom to move to another state without permission from the court and the noncustodial parent's right to continue his or her relationship with the child as established before the custodial parent's relocation.[1]

The Oklahoma Supreme Court also recognized the inherent conflict in the 2001 case of *Kaiser v. Kaiser*: "The interests of the custodial parent who desires to relocate and take the child to a new location and a new life are often in sharp conflict with those of the noncustodial parent who wants visitation and contact with the child to remain frequent and constant."[2]

Priority should be given to the primary custodial parent in relocation disputes.

When handing down decisions in relocation disputes, judges should give more consideration to the primary custodial parent.

This is the person who has given more of his or her time, money, energy, and life to care for his or her offspring. Usually, the custodial parent has a better relationship with the child involved than the noncustodial parent. The noncustodial parent may see the child far less frequently.

Social science research has concluded that children usually benefit more by continuity of custody in relocation situations than in switching households.[3] This research establishes that the child is best served by "remaining with the parent who actually does the day-to-day care and nurturing."[4] It is the primary caregiver who can protect the child best and shield him or her from the potentially damaging impacts of relocation. If the primary caregiver has provided a stable home environment, there is no need to uproot the child from that caregiver.[5] A number of state laws pertaining to child custody reflect this thinking. For example, Tennessee law provides that "the parent spending the greater amount of time with the child shall be permitted to relocate with the child" unless there are specific exceptions, such as that the move is not done for a reasonable purpose.[6]

A child's custodial parents have constitutional rights.

Whenever there is a relocation dispute, the constitutional rights of the custodial parents must be taken into consideration by courts. These rights include the constitutional right to travel, the right to rear their children as he or she sees fit, and the right to remarry, or marry, if he or she had not been previously married to the noncustodial parent.

The custodial parent should not have his or her fundamental right to travel impacted by a court that gives too much credence to the wishes of noncustodial parents. Individuals who are not involved in custodial disputes have the right to travel across the country as free citizens whenever they wish. Why should such an individual right be restricted by a judge during a custody dispute? If a court takes custody away from a custodial parent simply for moving—especially when all too often the parent

(continues on page 42)

Tennessee Code Annotated

Title 36 Domestic Relations
Chapter 6 Child Custody and Visitation
Part 1—General Custody Provisions
36-6-108. Parental relocation.

(1) If the parents are not actually spending substantially equal intervals of time with the child and the parent spending the greater amount of time with the child proposes to relocate with the child, the other parent may, within thirty (30) days of receipt of the notice, file a petition in opposition to the removal of the child. The other parent may not attempt to relocate with the child unless expressly authorized to do so by the court pursuant to a change of custody or primary custodial responsibility. The parent spending the greater amount of time with the child shall be permitted to relocate with the child unless the court finds:

(A) The relocation does not have a reasonable purpose;

(B) The relocation would pose a threat of specific and serious harm to the child that outweighs the threat of harm to the child of a change of custody; or

(C) The parent's motive for relocating with the child is vindictive in that it is intended to defeat or deter visitation rights of the noncustodial parent or the parent spending less time with the child.

(2) Specific and serious harm to the child includes, but is not limited to, the following:

(A) If a parent wishes to take a child with a serious medical problem to an area where no adequate treatment is readily available;

(B) If a parent wishes to take a child with specific educational requirements to an area with no acceptable education facilities;

(C) If a parent wishes to relocate and take up residence with a person with a history of child or domestic abuse or who is currently abusing alcohol or other drugs;

(D) If the child relies on the parent not relocating who provides emotional support, nurturing and development such that removal would result in severe emotional detriment to the child;

(E) If the custodial parent is emotionally disturbed or dependent such that the custodial parent is not capable of adequately parenting the child in the absence of support systems currently in place in this state, and such support system is not available at the proposed relocation site; or

(F) If the proposed relocation is to a foreign country whose public policy does not normally enforce the visitation rights of noncustodial parents, that does not have an adequately functioning legal system or that otherwise presents a substantial risk of specific and serious harm to the child. . . .

If the court finds it is not in the best interests of the child to relocate as defined herein, but the parent with whom the child resides the majority of the time elects to relocate, the court shall make a custody determination and shall consider all relevant factors including the following where applicable:

(1) The extent to which visitation rights have been allowed and exercised;

(2) Whether the primary residential parent, once out of the jurisdiction, is likely to comply with any new visitation arrangement;

(3) The love, affection and emotional ties existing between the parents and child;

(4) The disposition of the parents to provide the child with food, clothing, medical care, education and other necessary care and the degree to which a parent has been the primary caregiver;

(5) The importance of continuity in the child's life and the length of time the child has lived in a stable, satisfactory environment;

(6) The stability of the family unit of the parents;

(7) The mental and physical health of the parents;

(8) The home, school, and community record of the child;

(9) (A) The reasonable preference of the child if twelve (12) years of age or older;

(B) The court may hear the preference of a younger child upon request. The preferences of older children should normally be given greater weight than those of younger children;

(10) Evidence of physical or emotional abuse to the child, to the other parent or to any other person; and

(11) The character and behavior of any other person who resides in or frequents the home of a parent and such person's interactions with the child. . . .

Source: T.C.A. 36-1-108.

(continued from page 39)

moves simply for a better job opportunity—that court has violated the parent's constitutional rights. The South Carolina Supreme Court supported this argument when it ruled that "standards imposing restrictions on relocation have become antiquated in our increasingly transient society."[7]

Parents also have a constitutional right to rear their children as they see fit. Should a court violate that right without clear and compelling evidence that a child would be harmed by remaining

FROM THE BENCH

In Re Marriage of Burgess, 913 P.2d 473 (Cal. 1996)

In the case of *In Re Marriage of Burgess*, the California Supreme Court ruled on the fairness of parents' relocating in order to provide better opportunities for their children. The court wrote:

> Ours is an increasingly mobile society ... approximately one American in five changes residences each year. Economic necessity and remarriage account for the bulk of relocations. Because of the ordinary needs for both parents after a marital dissolution to secure or retain employment, pursue educational or career opportunities, or reside in the same location as a new spouse or other family or friends, it is unrealistic to assume that divorced parents will permanently remain in the same location after dissolution or to exert pressure on them to do so. . . .
>
> More fundamentally, the "necessity" of relocating frequently has little, if any, substantive bearing on the suitability of a parent to retain the role of a custodial parent. A parent who has been the primary caretaker for minor children is ordinarily no less capable of maintaining the responsibilities and obligations of parenting simply by virtue of a reasonable decision to change his or her geographical location. . . .
>
> Although this matter involved an initial order of custody and visitation, the same conclusion applies when a parent who has sole physical custody under an *existing* judicial custody order seeks to relocate: the custodial parent seeking to relocate, like the noncustodial parent doing the same, bears no burden of demonstrating that the move is "necessary."

with the custodial parent? If a custodial parent believes that a child's life would be dramatically improved by a move to a different location, he or she should be allowed to do so. Whenever a court prohibits a custodial parent from moving, the U.S. justice system has directly infringed upon this most fundamental right.

While there are many economic and social reasons for wanting to move to a new location—to better provide for a child, to give him or her greater educational opportunities— there are personal reasons as well. Often, custodial parents need to relocate in order to live with their new spouses. It would be not only illogical but also a great miscarriage of justice to prohibit a custodial parent from moving to another state to be with his or her new spouse. The North Dakota Supreme Court recognized this in the 2007 case of *Gilbert v. Gilbert*. In its decision, the court wrote: "When the custodial parent desires to live with a new spouse, we conclude that fact becomes dominant in favor of allowing the move, particularly, in cases such as this, when there is no evidence of ill motive or that the visitation is not likely to occur."[8]

The custodial parent should have presumption in favor of relocation.

Many state laws clearly favor a custodial parent's right to relocate. For example, California's Family law Code provides: "A parent entitled to the custody of a child has a right to change the residence of the child, subject to the power of the court to restrain a removal that would prejudice the rights or welfare of the child."[9] South Dakota passed a law with nearly identical language: "A parent entitled to the custody of a child has the right to change his residence, subject to the power of the circuit court to restrain a removal which would prejudice the rights or welfare of the child."[10] Other states have reached similar decisions in court decisions explaining such a statutory (legal) presumption. For example, the Oklahoma Supreme Court ruled in the 2001 case of *Kaiser v. Kaiser* that "in the absence of a showing of prejudice to the rights or welfare of a child, a custodial parent has a statutory presumptive right to change their child's residence."[11] Looking at the growing number of states with such language in their family law codes, it is clear that courts nationwide should not interfere with a custodial parent's decision to improve the quality of his or her life and that of the child unless there is a vindictive reason for the move.

There are other ways for children to keep contact with noncustodial parents.

Our era has often been called the "information age" because we live in a vastly interconnected world. Modern technological advancements have provided many opportunities for noncustodial parents to maintain contact with children even when a custodial parent relocates. There is e-mail, telephone, social media, and video conferencing available for continued and

FROM THE BENCH

Gilbert v. Gilbert, 730 N.W.2d 833 (N.D. 2007)

In the case of *Gilbert v. Gilbert*, the North Dakota Supreme Court recognized the important role virtual visitation could play in custody disputes. The following is an excerpt from the court's decision:

> Virtual visitation includes using the telephone, Internet, web-cam, and other wireless or wired technologies to ensure the child has frequent and meaningful contact with the noncustodial parent. It is most useful in cases such as this where the child and noncustodial parent are accustomed to seeing each other on a regular basis but no longer will be able to because of the relocation. Virtual visitation is not a substitute for personal contact, but it can be a useful tool to supplement in-person visitation. Virtual visitation is becoming more widely recognized as a way to supplement in-person visitation.

Michael Gough stands behind his computer in Brookfield, Wisconsin, with his daughter Saige on the monitor, in February 2006. Gough is on the forefront of a movement to get more states to guarantee that divorced parents can have "virtual visitation" rights in custody cases.

regular contact with noncustodial parents. In fact, the video conferencing option is part of a new movement called "virtual visitation," which helps to maintain regular personal contact between a parent and child remotely.[12] Courts are recognizing that virtual visitation can help alleviate the problems by lack of physical contact. In addition to this form of visitation, the non-custodial parent could have longer periods of physical visitation during the summers and holidays to offset the losses suffered by out-of-state moves by the custodial parent.

Summary

Primary custodial parents should have the option of relocating to another city or state in order to provide better economic, social, or educational opportunities for themselves and their children. The reasoning for this is simple: Primary custodial parents shoulder the bulk of the burden in rearing their children and can best make decisions for them. Unless the relocation move is done for a vindictive or illegitimate reason, the courts should allow such relocation liberally. Restricting the primary custodial parents from freely moving infringes upon many of the parents' constitutional rights, including the rights to travel and marry freely.

In today's society, which enables parents and children to communicate from virtually anywhere and at any time, it is illogical to force custodial and noncustodial parents to remain in the same geographic location so that the children they share can see each parent regularly. There are other ways for the non-custodial parent to maintain sufficient contact with the parent, including various forms of virtual visitation and longer periods of visitation during the summer months and during holiday schedules.

The Interests of the Noncustodial Parent Should Be Given Greater Protection

A man and a woman marry and have a child. For a few years, the marriage works well and the family unit remains intact. Then the relationship between the husband and wife deteriorates and they agree to divorce. The child's mother receives primary physical custody, but the father receives a healthy amount of visitation—weekends, summers, and many holidays. This allows the parties' child to have regular contact with both parents, helping to ease the tensions from a difficult situation.

The mother, however, is offered a better job in another state and moves there with the child. The mother and child now live in a state that provides virtually no protection for the father, who is not the primary custodial parent. The state law presumes that the mother has a valid and good reason for moving to the other state. As a result of the move, the father has lost substantial opportunities to bond with his own child.

When the father contests the move in court, the trial judge says that the father should be placated by the availability of video conferencing and other forms of virtual visitation. The father counters that such methods, although a nice supplement, simply do not afford the same type of connection that a real-life visitation provides.

As this theoretical case illustrates, noncustodial parents are too often slighted when the custodial parent moves to another city or state. The relocation dilemma becomes even more complicated when the parties involved have a version of joint custody. In a joint custody arrangement, one party may be awarded primary physical custody, but both parents are supposed to be jointly involved in the major life decisions impacting the child—and that requires each parent to live in close proximity to his or her children.

Both courts and state laws should make it harder for parents to relocate.

In some states, it is far too easy for custodial parents to pack up and move their children away from the noncustodial parents, whose bonds with their children will be shattered. Often the loss of those key emotional bonds can serve as a detriment to a child who, unable to maintain the close personal contact with both parents, may suffer developmentally. Unfortunately, in such states, the law allows this too easily.

Fortunately, in many other states, courts employ tougher standards when evaluating the petitions of relocating parents. The Supreme Court of New Jersey denied the request by a father—the primary custodial parent—to move with his child from New Jersey to Florida. The father wished to move for a better employment opportunity. The move, however, would disrupt the mother's visitation schedule and deprive her of the opportunity to see her child. The Supreme Court of New Jersey took into account the fact that the mother did not have the financial resources to travel to Florida to see her child. Because the child's bonds with the mother would be harmed, the trial court deemed that the move would not be in the best interest of the child. The state's supreme court agreed.[1]

Laws across the United States should be amended to place the burden of proof on the relocating parent that the move is made for legitimate reasons and actually benefits the child. Otherwise, a parent who maintains primary custody will be able to relocate over the legitimate objections of the other parent. One legal commentator mentions the following model law: "The relocating parent has the burden of proof that the proposed relocation is made in good faith and in the best interest of the child."[2] Illinois' current relocation law is close to this type. It provides: "The relocating individual has the burden of proof that the proposed relocation is made in good faith and for a legitimate reason."[3] Alabama's law creates a rebuttable presumption that a relocation move by a parent is not in the best interests of the child.[4]

In the 2006 case of *Toler v. Toler*, an Alabama appeals court ruled that the state's proposed relocation law allows custody to be switched if the custodial parent moves the child away and infringes upon the rights of the noncustodial parent and against the best interests of the child. In the *Toler* case, the parties' minor son was able to see both parents regularly because the divorced parties lived very close to each other. Then the mother moved with her new husband to an area that required her young son to be taken from his school, his father, and his friends—all familiar parts of his life. By making the move, the appeals court recognized that "the mother uprooted the approximately 14-year-old son from his home, his friends, his school, his church and his other day-to-day activities and contacts."[5] The court explained that changing the primary custody to the father would "have left much of the son's day-to-day life intact and would have been less disruptive to the son than leaving custody with the mother."[6]

This court concluded that the legal system should carefully consider the interests of the child when a custodial parent relocates, uprooting a child from the child's settled routine. It often is in the child's best interest to remain in his or her current situation, going to the same school, church, and other activities.

THE LETTER OF THE LAW

Alabama's Law on Relocation in Child Custody Cases

Upon the entry of a temporary order or upon final judgment permitting the change of principal residence of a child, a court may consider a proposed change of principal residence of a child as a factor to support a change of custody of the child. In determining whether a proposed or actual change of principal residence of a minor child should cause a change in custody of that child, a court shall take into account all factors affecting the child, including, but not limited to, the following:

(1) The nature, quality, extent of involvement, and duration of the child's relationship with the person proposing to relocate with the child and with the non-relocating person, siblings, and other significant persons or institutions in the child's life.

(2) The age, developmental stage, needs of the child, and the likely impact the change of principal residence of a child will have on the child's physical, educational, and emotional development, taking into consideration any special needs of the child.

(3) The increase in travel time for the child created by the change in principal residence of the child or a person entitled to custody of or visitation with the child.

(4) The availability and cost of alternate means of communication between the child and the non-relocating party.

(5) The feasibility of preserving the relationship between the non-relocating person and the child through suitable visitation arrangements, considering the logistics and financial circumstances of the parties.

(6) The preference of the child, taking into consideration the age and maturity of the child.

(7) The degree to which a change or proposed change of the principal residence of the child will result in uprooting the child as compared to the degree to which a modification of the custody of the child will result in uprooting the child.

It would be wise for courts in other states to come to similar conclusions and therefore provide blanket security to both children and parents.

(8) The extent to which custody and visitation rights have been allowed and exercised.

(9) Whether there is an established pattern of conduct of the person seeking to change the principal residence of a child, either to promote or thwart the relationship of the child and the non-relocating person.

(10) Whether the person seeking to change the principal residence of a child, once out of the jurisdiction, is likely to comply with any new visitation arrangement and the disposition of that person to foster a joint parenting arrangement with the non-relocating party.

(11) Whether the relocation of the child will enhance the general quality of life for both the custodial party seeking the change of principal residence of the child and for the child, including, but not limited to, financial or emotional benefit or educational opportunities.

(12) Whether or not a support system is available in the area of the proposed new residence of the child, especially in the event of an emergency or disability to the person having custody of the child.

(13) Whether or not the proposed new residence of a child is to a foreign country whose public policy does not normally enforce the visitation rights of noncustodial parents, which does not have an adequately functioning legal system, or which otherwise presents a substantial risk of specific and serious harm to the child.

(14) The stability of the family unit of the persons entitled to custody of and visitation with a child.

(15) The reasons of each person for seeking or opposing a change of principal residence of a child.

(16) Evidence relating to a history of domestic violence or child abuse.

(17) Any other factor that in the opinion of the court is material to the general issue or otherwise provided by law.

Source: Ala. Code § 30-3-169.3.

Relocation often harms children.

According to legal commentator Elisabeth Bach-Van Horn, "Regrettably, relocation is all-too-often viewed from the parents' perspectives: one parent's right to move is pitted against the other parent's right to a continuing relationship with the child."[7] This focus on parental rights—instead of on children's rights—is particularly unfortunate in light of the fact that much of the social science literature on the subject clearly establishes that relocation often harms children. Psychologist and author William G. Austin reports that "relocation for children of divorce, like divorce itself, stands as a general risk factor for long-term behavioral outcomes and informs evaluators and decision makers about a base rate of harm associated with relocation for children of divorce."[8] Austin explains that relocation is bad enough for any child, but that these negative effects are multiplied for children who are relocated because of divorce. He explains that such children have higher dropout rates and an increased likelihood of poor academic performance, premarital childbearing, and drug abuse. He adds that "when divorce and residential mobility are both entered into regression equations, then there is a strong effect on educational outcomes."[9] At another point in his article, Austin explains that "if divorce and relocation temporarily co-occur, then it follows that the child is at the greatest level of risk."[10]

Because relocation often harms children, the courts should consider the reasonable preferences of the child in making custody determinations. In many state laws, the reasonable preference of the child is listed as a permissible factor in determining child custody cases. More states should consider the preferences of children when one parent relocates to provide national uniformity to such laws and to prevent more children from suffering disruptions in their lives.

Virtual visitation is no substitute
for actual physical contact.

More and more courts are allowing relocation for the primary custodial parent in part because of the availability of virtual visitation. This is a mistake, as virtual visitation is not a replacement for physical contact. Parenting remotely does not allow the noncustodial spouse and the child to have a real and meaningful relationship. Legal commentator Elisabeth Bach-Van Horn explains: "The internet can be an instrument for a 'face-to-face' encounter between parent and child, but video-conferencing with one's child, just like a telephone call, should be used as a supplement to, not a replacement for, in-person visits and communication."[11]

While states have begun passing laws allowing for various forms of electronic communication or virtual visitation, these laws specifically say that such forms of communication should not be used as a substitute for physical contact. For example,

QUOTABLE

Legal commentator Elisabeth Bach-Van Horn

Virtual visitation is gaining popularity and, as indicated by the large number of states with plans for allowing such visitation to be ordered by statute, it's not likely to disappear. The good news is that each state that has proposed a bill thus far to allow incorporation of virtual visitation into parenting plans has also included a provision stating that this alternative visitation is not to be used to replace physical visitation. The bad news is that the mandate to use virtual visitation as a supplement to, and not a substitute for, regular visitation cannot be regulated with any degree of certainty; using this language does not remove the possibilities for abuse of the alternative visitation by parents or judges.

Many debates have arisen over the benefits and detriments of virtual visitation. The one thing that everyone seems to agree on is that regardless of the internet's convenience and efficiency, and the many wonderful tools that have been invented to bring two people closer no matter how far they are physically distanced, the internet will never be capable of fulfilling all of the many benefits of physical interaction between a parent and child.

Source: Elisabeth Bach-Van Horn, "Virtual Visitation: Are Webcams Being Used as an Excuse to Allow Relocation?" 21 *Journal of the American Academy of Matrimonial Lawyers* 171, 192 (2008).

Florida's law provides: "Electronic communication may be used only to supplement a parent's face-to-face contact with his or her minor child. Electronic communication may not be used to replace or as a substitute for face-to-face contact."[12] North

THE LETTER OF THE LAW

An Excerpt from the North Carolina Law on Electronic Communication and Child Custody

(e) An order for custody of a minor child may provide for visitation rights by electronic communication. In granting visitation by electronic communication, the court shall consider the following:

(1) Whether electronic communication is in the best interest of the minor child.

(2) Whether equipment to communicate by electronic means is available, accessible, and affordable to the parents of the minor child.

(3) Any other factor the court deems appropriate in determining whether to grant visitation by electronic communication.

The court may set guidelines for electronic communication, including the hours in which the communication may be made, the allocation of costs between the parents in implementing electronic communication with the child, and the furnishing of access information between parents necessary to facilitate electronic communication. Electronic communication with a minor child may be used to supplement visitation with the child. Electronic communication may not be used as a replacement or substitution for custody or visitation. The amount of time electronic communication is used shall not be a factor in calculating child support or be used to justify or support relocation by the custodial parent out of the immediate area or the State. Electronic communication between the minor child and the parent may be subject to supervision as ordered by the court. As used in this subsection, "electronic communication" means contact, other than face-to-face contact, facilitated by electronic means, such as by telephone, electronic mail, instant messaging, video teleconferencing, wired or wireless technologies by Internet, or other medium of communication.

Source: N.C.G.S.A. § 50-13.2(e).

Carolina's law explains that electronic communication shall not be used as a consideration as to whether relocation is available to a parent. "The amount of time electronic communication is used shall not be a factor in calculating child support or be used to justify or support relocation by the custodial parent out of the immediate area or the state," the law reads.[13]

Summary

Too many states' child custody laws make it easy for custodial parents to relocate. Such laws focus too much on the economic interests of the custodial parent and not enough on the needs of the child. Relocations often disrupt the lives of children, in turn destroying not only the visitation schedules of noncustodial parents but also negatively impacting the lives of the children, who need regular routines and personal contact with both parents in order to grow into well-adjusted adults. To counteract this growing problem, courts should create rebuttable presumptions that require custodial parents to justify their relocations with legitimate reasons in a legal setting.

For the children of divorce, relocation often has very negative effects upon their lives. These kids often do more poorly in school than the children of parents who did not divorce or relocate and frequently do not adjust very well to these moves. They are also at greater risk for all sorts of antisocial behaviors. Therefore, courts should not allow virtual visitation to be used as a substitute for actual, physical, face-to-face visitation. There is no substitute for the familial bonds established between children and both parents—not simply the parent who is the day-to-day primary caregiver.

Race Should Not Be a Factor in Child Custody Decisions

An interracial couple marries and wants to start a family. The couple has a child, fulfilling the wishes and dreams of both parents. Unfortunately, the marital relationship breaks down and the parties eventually enter into a contested divorce. The mother and father engage in a bitter custody dispute. The mother, who is black, asserts in the custody dispute that her biracial child should live with her because she is the better and more stable parent and because society will perceive the biracial child as black. The father, who is white, counters that he is the more stable parent and is better able to financially provide for the child. Because the trial court finds that both parties are good and fit parents, the decision comes down to the question of race. Racial identity, the judge agrees, is an important consideration that must be taken into account. The trial court then awards custody of the child to the mother. Even though the father may be an equally qualified parent and despite the fact that the child may be financially better off with him, race proves to be the deciding factor.

One would think that in the United States in the early twenty-first century, our society would have progressed closer to a color-blind society, especially in light of the fact that the country elected its first African-American president in 2008. Unfortunately, the ideal of a color-blind society does not match the reality of racial divisiveness and even abject racism that continues to exist. Many in this world still judge people by their racial identity. While this is unfortunate, the judicial system should not cater to it by considering race as a relevant factor in child custody cases.

The U.S. Supreme Court has condemned the use of race in child custody decisions.

In the 1984 case of *Palmore v. Sidoti*, the United States Supreme Court overruled the use of race in child custody disputes that had been regularly employed by some lower courts.[1] In this case, Linda Sidoti Palmore and Anthony J. Sidoti were two Caucasian individuals who married. The couple had a young daughter. After the parties divorced, the mother was awarded custody of the child. The father, however, challenged the custody award in part on the basis of race. He contended that his ex-wife's cohabitation and eventual marriage to Clarence Palmore Jr., a black man, was a negative factor. Anthony argued that the young daughter would face negative comments from her peers at school and otherwise suffer adverse effects from her mother's interracial marriage.[2] The Florida trial judge agreed with this argument, writing:

> The Court feels that despite the strides that have been made in bettering relations between the races in this country, it is inevitable that Melanie will, if allowed to remain in her present situation and attains school age and thus more vulnerable to peer pressures, suffer from the social stigmatization that is sure to come.[3]

The case eventually reached the U.S. Supreme Court, where the decision was unanimously reversed. Chief Justice Warren Burger determined that the Equal Protection Clause of the Fourteenth Amendment provides a very high standard for the government to justify any type of racial classification. Generally, any type of race-based classification must pass strict scrutiny, the highest and most stringent form of judicial review. In the context of this case, Burger noted that it was clear that race was the sole factor used by the trial court in changing custody to the father. "Taking the court's findings and rationale at face value, it is clear that the outcome would have been different had

FROM THE BENCH

Palmore v. Sidoti, 466 U.S. 429 (1984)

The [Florida] court correctly stated that the child's welfare was the controlling factor. But that court was entirely candid and made no effort to place its holding on any ground other than race. Taking the court's findings and rationale at face value, it is clear that the outcome would have been different had petitioner married a Caucasian male of similar respectability.

A core purpose of the Fourteenth Amendment was to do away with all governmentally imposed discrimination based on race. . . . Classifying persons according to their race is more likely to reflect racial prejudice than legitimate public concerns; the race, not the person, dictates the category. . . . Such classifications are subject to the most exacting scrutiny; to pass constitutional muster, they must be justified by a compelling governmental interest and must be "necessary . . . to the accomplishment" of their legitimate purpose.

The State, of course, has a duty of the highest order to protect the interests of minor children, particularly those of tender years. In common with most states, Florida law mandates that custody determinations be made in the best interests of the children involved. . . . The goal of granting custody based on the best interests of the child is indisputably a substantial governmental interest for purposes of the Equal Protection Clause.

petitioner [Linda Sidoti Palmore] married a Caucasian male of similar respectability."[4] Chief Justice Burger concluded that "the effects of racial prejudice, however real, cannot justify a racial classification removing an infant child from the custody of its natural mother found to be an appropriate person to have such custody."[5]

In 1981, three years prior to this U.S. Supreme Court ruling, a New York court reached a similar conclusion in the case of *Farmer v. Farmer*.[6] Linda Farmer, a white woman, and Billie Farmer, a black man, together had a child named Bethany. The parties eventually divorced and entered into a custody dispute.

It would ignore reality to suggest that racial and ethnic prejudices do not exist or that all manifestations of those prejudices have been eliminated. There is a risk that a child living with a stepparent of a different race may be subject to a variety of pressures and stresses not present if the child were living with parents of the same racial or ethnic origin.

The question, however, is whether the reality of private biases and the possible injury they might inflict are permissible considerations for removal of an infant child from the custody of its natural mother. We have little difficulty concluding that they are not. The Constitution cannot control such prejudices but neither can it tolerate them. Private biases may be outside the reach of the law, but the law cannot, directly or indirectly, give them effect. . . .

This is by no means the first time that acknowledged racial prejudice has been invoked to justify racial classifications. In *Buchanan v. Warley*, . . . (1917), for example, . . . this Court invalidated a Kentucky law forbidding Negroes to buy homes in white neighborhoods. . . .

Whatever problems racially mixed households may pose for children in 1984 can no more support a denial of constitutional rights than could the stresses that residential integration was thought to entail in 1917. The effects of racial prejudice, however real, cannot justify a racial classification removing an infant child from the custody of its natural mother found to be an appropriate person to have such custody.

Mixed-race marriage in U.S.

The number of people marrying someone of a different race has increased dramatically in recent decades. A look at the latest data:

By race and ethnicity

Percent with spouse
of a different race, 2000:

White	3.1%
Black	5.7%
Asian	16.3%
Hispanic	16.3%

By sex

Percent with spouse
of a different race, 2000:

	Male	Female
White	3.4%	2.9%
Black	8.1%	3.2%
Asian	10.6%	21.4%
Hispanic	15.1%	17.2%

Since 1960

Total number of married couples
and interracial couples:

	All couples	Interracial
1960	40.5 million	149,000
1980	49.5 million	953,000
2000	56.5 million*	1.5 million**

*From 2000 Current Population Survey
**From 1999 Current Population Survey;
most recent number available; does not
count the estimated 1.5 million Hispanic
intermarriages
NOTE: Hispanics can be of any race

© 2001 KRT
SOURCE: U.S. Census Bureau's Current
Population Survey, Decennial Census;
William H. Frey, Milken Institute
Research/JUDY TREIBLE

The percent of interracial marriage has been on the rise in the United States in recent decades. These statistics are taken from the 2000 census, the last one publicly available as of this writing. It is projected that these numbers rose further in the 2010 census. Race is often a key factor in helping to determine child custody.

The father asserted that his biracial daughter should live with him because he was African-American and Bethany would be considered as African-American by society. Several experts testified as to the problems that biracial children face in society. "Social and psychological problems can result from the unresolved internal conflicts which are the product of confused identity," the court wrote.[7]

Even though the New York court recognized these potential problems that biracial children may face, the court rejected the father's argument that children must live with the parent of the same considered race in society: "The defendant father's thesis—that the best interests of this child of an interracial marriage compel the award of custody to him because society will perceive her to be black—must be rejected."[8]

Courts in other states, however, are not obligated to follow the *Farmer* ruling, and unfortunately, the racial question still arises in custody disputes. Consider the case of *Tipton v. Aaron* (2004).[9] In this case, two white minors, Mellisa Tipton and Zeb Aaron, had a child named Colten. Tipton's parents obtained custody of the child and then later wanted to transfer custody to their daughter. Aaron contested this and sought custody for himself. Later Mellisa married a biracial man and had a child with him.

Zeb Aaron contended that he did not want his child placed in a home with a half-black stepfather and "interracial things." He did not think it would be fair to his child because of "what he's going to hear growing up and everything he is going to be around."[10] He later testified that he "did not believe in the interracial thing and the mixing" and that "some people accept it, but it's not right." He said that his son would be considered the "oddball."[11] A trial court awarded custody to Zeb Aaron, despite the fact that he had a criminal record and past drug problems. On appeal, however, the Arkansas Court of Appeals reversed the lower court ruling. The appeals court concluded:

In examining this evidence, we hold that the trial court was clearly erroneous in awarding custody of the child to Zeb, and that it would be in his best interests for custody to be placed with Mellisa. It is clear that Mellisa has had more direct involvement in the day-to-day care and financial support of Colten. She is married to a man who has a good relationship with Colten and who has a good job. They live close to her parents, who have served as Colten's guardians his entire life. Moreover, they live in a diverse community, where interracial households are not unusual. Furthermore, Mellisa's child-rearing philosophy promotes racial tolerance, while Zeb's does not.[12]

THE LETTER OF THE LAW

Puerto Rico Law on Best Interests of Children

The public policy of the Government of Puerto Rico seeks to uphold and guarantee the rights of children and the respect of their dignity. By so providing, we hereby take into account the variable degree of vulnerability to which children are subject during their process of development and socialization, until they attain full legal standing, and the State's responsibility to provide the means and resources needed to safeguard their interests and advance their welfare.

All measures concerning children as well as all interventions of the State involving the powers and authority germane to *patria potestas* or guardianship, shall have as their guiding principle the protection of the family as an institution, and the best interests and welfare of children, taking into consideration the degree of development of their capabilities, and free from any discrimination motivated by origin, race, color, birth [sic], political or religious beliefs, disabilities, sex, socioeconomic or cultural status of the children, or for any other personal consideration. The State recognizes that the parents or guardians are primarily responsible for the control, supervision, and guidance of their children.

Source: P.R. Laws Ann. tit. 1, § 421.

Tragically, some courts have sanctioned the use of race as a consideration in child custody decisions. An Illinois appeals court in the 2006 case of *In Re Marriage of Gambla* ruled that race was a key deciding factor in deciding to place primary custody of a biracial child with her black mother as opposed to her white father. "The cold reality is that no one can put blindfolds on in this case," the court wrote. "Christopher [the father] is Caucasian, Kimberly [the mother] is African-American, and Kira [the child] is biracial. Illinois case law provides that race may be considered, but that it may not outweigh all of the other relevant factors."[13] A dissenting judge criticized the majority for "erroneously us[ing] race as its basis for awarding custody."[14]

Race should not be considered in best interests statutes.

State child custody laws generally articulate that primary custody should be determined based on the best interests of the child. Many state laws list numerous factors that courts may consider in making this key determination that will greatly impact children's lives. Common factors include the relationship of the child to the current primary caretaker, the mental and physical health of the parents, and the reasonable preference of the child above a certain age. No state in its statute allows race to be considered as a predominant factor in making child custody determinations. Some state laws, however, specifically forbid the consideration of race in custody and child placement considerations. For example, Wisconsin law provides: "The court may not prefer one potential custodian over the other on the basis of the sex or race of the custodian."[15]

Yet some codes do not go far enough. They seem to imply that race can be a factor in child custody determinations. For example, a District of Columbia law provides: "In any proceeding between parents in which the custody of a child is raised as an issue, the best interest of the child shall be the primary consideration. The race, color . . . in and of itself, shall not be a conclusive consideration."[16] Related family law statutes preclude the consideration of race. A Minnesota law dealing with the placement of children in foster care provides: "Placement of a child cannot be delayed or denied based on race, color, or national origin of the foster parent or child."[17]

In the adoption arena, the U.S. Congress made a considerable stride forward when it passed the Multiethnic Placement Act in 1994. This law prohibits delaying or denying the placement of children or denying someone the chance to be a foster or adoptive parent on the basis of race. Originally the act prohibiting delaying or denying adoptions based "solely" on race. In 1996, however, Congress amended the law to remove the word "solely," making it harder to deny transracial adoptions.[18] Several states have similar laws. For example, Missouri's law provides: "Placement of a child in an adoptive home may not be delayed or denied on the basis of race, color or national origin."[19]

Many studies have established that children do very well in multiracial families.[20] The number of transracial adoptions has skyrocketed in recent years. Studies of families that have adopted children of other races have been nearly uniformly positive.[21] This shows that the best interest of children should not include a consideration of race.

Removing race from the child custody arena moves us closer to being a color-blind society.

A primary goal of the Equal Protection Clause of the Fourteenth Amendment is to ensure equality in society. If a person of one race is treated differently than a person of another race, the specter of discrimination rears its ugly head. For centuries, rank racial discrimination persisted in American society, beginning with the "peculiar institution" of slavery up to various Jim Crow segregation laws that were finally abolished in the 1960s. Now that legal racial discrimination has been abolished, it is important that our legal system insure that de facto racial prejudice be abolished as well. The ultimate goal of a just and fair society should be to eliminate all vestiges of discrimination in order to achieve a truly color-blind society.

There is no way to achieve a color-blind, discrimination-free society if the legal system sanctions race-based preferences in the child custody arena. To say that a child's best interests in a custody dispute can be based on race injects the idea that one race is better than another, that being with one parent because of his or her skin color is more beneficial to the child than being with the other. Parents should be judged on the quality of their parenting skills, not on the color of their skin.

Summary

Children should be placed with the parent who can provide the most loving, caring environment for them. They should be placed with the parent with whom they have the deepest emotional connection and relationship. In short, children in child custody disputes should be placed with the best parents under the circumstances and not for any mitigating reasons like race. The U.S. Supreme Court has determined that placing a child based on race can violate the Equal Protection Clause of the Fourteenth Amendment. For this reason, many state courts and legislatures have forbidden or limited the use of race as a criterion in child custody cases. The law should evolve even further and not only prohibit race as the sole or dominant factor in child custody, but also flatly prohibit any consideration of race in child custody cases. This should be the norm across the United States, because our society has been working bit by bit toward becoming a color-blind society since the end of the Civil War in 1865. Parents should be judged by the quality of their parenting, not by the color of their skin. There will be no way to get past the vestiges of racism and discrimination in American society if child custody laws keep discriminating against some parents based on race.

Race Is a Valid Concern in Child Custody Disputes

A child is born to biracial parents, a black mother and a white father. Society, however, regards this child as African-American. That fact is undeniable. The reality, as one legal commentator has noted, is that "children with black and white parents have been classified as black by both society and law."[1] When a biracial child of a black-white union has to check a box when filling out a form, they often fill out the form "African-American" or "black." This is the reality of the color line that has dominated American society since its inception.

Race matters in child custody cases, too. When a couple divorces, the child will be placed with one of the two parents. In the case of an interracial marriage between a Caucasian man and an African-American mother, the mother often may be better able to relate to the societal discrimination that the child will endure than the Caucasian father.

In child custody law, the court must consider the best interest of the child. In awarding custody, a judge must weigh the emotional bonds between each parent, the ability of the respective parents to provide for the child, and the reasonable preference of the child. Equally relevant—as important as any one of the others in the custody decision—is race. American society is not color blind. Prejudices continue to endure, despite legal prohibitions against them. Therefore, if society considers race, so too should the courts, especially in custody disputes. Race should not be the sole factor, but it should be a key consideration in the ultimate decision.

The U.S. Supreme Court only prohibited race as the *sole* factor in custody disputes.

The U.S. Supreme Court in *Palmore v. Sidoti* (1984) did rule that racial prejudice was an impermissible reason to remove a child from his mother *solely* because of the factor of race. In *Palmore*, the Court overruled a trial court decision to remove a child from Linda Sidoti's home because she cohabitated with and later married an African-American man. Sidoti's former husband, who was father to her child, objected to their daughter living in an interracial home. The trial court judge focused on the race factor to the exclusion of other factors. The Supreme Court determined that this was not only impermissible but was also a violation of the Equal Protection Clause of the Fourteenth Amendment, which provides that people should be treated equally.

Although the high court's ruling means that race cannot be the sole or predominant factor in a custody decision, it does not mean that race cannot, or should not, play a role at all in the custody decision. In its decision, the U.S. Supreme Court focused on the fact that the trial judge's ruling obsessed about race: "But that court was entirely candid and made no effort to place its holding on any ground other than race. Taking the court's findings and rationale at face value, it is clear that the outcome would have been different had petitioner married a Caucasian male of similar respectability."[2]

The Court also noted that "there is a risk that a child living with a stepparent of a different race may be subject to a variety of pressures and stresses not present if the child were living with parents of the same racial or ethnic origin."[3] Despite changes in society and in many laws, many believe that such reasoning holds true today.

Other courts have recognized that race can be a factor in custody decisions.

In the 2006 case of *In Re Marriage of Gambla,* an Illinois appeals court agreed that race can be one factor among many—even a deciding factor that tilts the balance—in a child custody case.[4] The Illinois appeals court granted custody of a biracial child named Kira to her African-American mother, Kimberly Newsome, rather than to her Caucasian father, Christopher Gambla, in part because of race and racial identity. Crucial to this determination was its interpretation of the Supreme Court's *Palmore* decision as prohibiting race as the only factor in rendering a child custody determination: "The Supreme Court [in *Palmore*] determined that the custody award was unconstitutional, not because the trial court considered race, but because the trial court considered *solely* race."[5]

A Nebraska appeals court also recognized that race can be an important factor in child custody determinations as long as it is not the only factor. In *Ebirim v. Ebirim,* the court wrote that "race is but one factor to be considered in custody determinations."[6] Minnesota law allows courts to consider the "child's cultural background" in determining the best interests of the child.[7] Such laws may be particularly relevant in states where Native American tribes are trying to preserve their cultural heritage.

In 1996, the South Dakota Supreme Court ruled in *Jones v. Jones* that it was permissible for a trial court judge to consider race and ethnicity in awarding primary custody to a Native

American father who had been in an interracial marriage with a Caucasian female. The Court explained that "it is proper for a trial court, when determining the best interests of a child in the

FROM THE BENCH

Jones v. Jones, 542 N.W.2d 119 (S.D. 1996)

[The plaintiff] Dawn [R. Jones] argues that the trial court awarded the children to [her former husband] Kevin [Mark Jones] for the principal reason that, as a Native American, he has suffered prejudice and will therefore be able to better deal with the needs of the children when they are discriminated against because, although they are biracial, they have Native American features. She contends that the trial court impermissibly considered the matter of race when determining the custody of the children and thereby violated her right to equal ... protection of the laws as found in Section One of the Fourteenth Amendment to the United States Constitution.

In support of her arguments, Dawn cites to the decision of the United States Supreme Court in *Palmore v. Sidoti*.... In *Palmore*, the mother and father were both Caucasian. They divorced and the mother was awarded custody of their minor daughter. The mother subsequently lived with and then married a Negro man which prompted the father to sue for change of custody. The trial court changed custody solely and expressly because the child was likely to experience discrimination if she remained in a biracial household. The Supreme Court reversed. In doing so it recognized that, while the child may well experience prejudice because she lived in a biracial home and that her best interests might be served by a change of custody, "[t]he effects of racial prejudice, however real, cannot justify a racial classification removing an infant child from the custody of its natural mother found to be an appropriate person to have such custody." ... The rationale for this holding was that although the constitution cannot control racial and other ethnic prejudices, "neither can it tolerate them. Private biases may be outside the reach of the law, but the law cannot, directly or indirectly, give them effect." ...

Albeit the trial court did not cite to *Palmore* in either its memorandum opinion (which was incorporated into its findings and conclusions) or in the findings of fact and conclusions of law, the court was apparently aware of its

context of a custody dispute between parents, to consider the matter of race as it relates to a child's ethnic heritage and which parent is more prepared to expose the child to it."[8]

holding and scrupulously honored it. The trial court wrote in the memorandum opinion:

Plaintiff addressed the issue of racial discrimination and Native American culture in his testimony. He states that all three children would be discriminated against as Native Americans if they left Penrhos farm to live. He wants for them the same loving, non-discriminatory upbringing that he received as a child at Penrhos. Plaintiff also wants to continue to make the children aware of their culture and heritage and participate in Tribal functions. . . . This is an example of the Plaintiff's concern for the totality of the upbringing of his children. However, this Court's determination of custody must be made on a racially neutral basis as far as concerning itself with the effects of any potential discrimination. . . .

Also in finding number 27 of the findings of fact and conclusions of law prepared by Kevin's counsel, the trial court deleted the portion that stated that the children would be subject to discrimination if they were raised away from Penrhos Farms and handwrote that "[c]ustody determinations are to be made on a racially neutral basis.". . .

While the trial court was not blind to the racial backgrounds of the children, we are satisfied that it did not impermissibly award custody on the basis of race. As noted, Kevin showed sensitivity to the need for his children to be exposed to their ethnic heritage. All of us form our own personal identities, based in part, on our religious, racial, and cultural backgrounds. To say, as Dawn argues, that a court should never consider whether a parent is willing and able to expose to and educate children on their heritage, is to say that society is not interested in whether children ever learn who they are. *Palmore* does not require this, nor do the constitutions . . . of the United States or the State of South Dakota. We hold that it is proper for a trial court, when determining the best interests of a child in the context of a custody dispute between parents, to consider the matter of race as it relates to a child's ethnic heritage and which parent is more prepared to expose the child to it.

Racial identity of a child is a permissible factor in child custody determinations.

Having an individual identity is important for any person, especially a child who is coming up in the world. The South Dakota Supreme Court explained in *Jones v. Jones* (1996) that "all of us form our own personal identities, based in part, on our religious, racial and cultural backgrounds."[9] Children are no different, as they base part of their personal identity on religion, race, and/or culture. These are important factors in a child's development. It ignores reality to discount the fact that one parent—because of his or her race or culture—may not be able to better serve the child in determining their identity.

In the *Gambla* case, the Illinois appeals court and the Illinois trial court below both credited the testimony of Dr. Anita Thomas, a psychologist who has published widely on racial and cultural matters. Dr. Thomas testified that the court should take into account the child's biracial identity and award custody to the African-American mother. Dr. Thomas explained that it was important for the child to be socialized in the African-American culture and that she would get a better sense of her racial identity from her mother.[10] The Illinois appeals court candidly wrote: "The cold reality is that no one can put blindfolds on in this case. Christopher is Caucasian, Kimberly is African-American, and Kira is biracial. Illinois case law provides that race may be considered, but that it may not outweigh all of the other relevant factors."[11]

Because racial identity is so important culturally, some groups are now advocating that race should again play a factor in adoptions. In 1994, Congress passed the Multiethnic Placement Act, which provided that race could not be the sole factor in an adoption decision. However, in 1996, Congress amended the law and removed the word "solely." This change in the law has had some detrimental impact on minority children.

The Evan B. Donaldson Adoption Institute in its report "Finding Families for African American Children" contends that the law should revert back to the 1994 version and allow race to be one factor among many in adoption law. "Federal law must strike an appropriate balance between the prevention of discriminatory conduct and the rational consideration of a child's racial/ethnic identity needs," the report reads. "Law should be congruent with practice, directing that the matching process address the ability of a family to meet all of a child's needs, including racial/ethnic identity and socialization."[12]

The study also found that racial identity was particularly important to African-American children, the focus for the institute. The study also cited other research that found that "black children had a greater sense of racial pride when their parents acknowledged racial identity, moved to integrated neighborhoods, and provided African American role models. Black children whose white parents minimized the importance of racial identity were reluctant to identify themselves racially."[13]

Summary

Race and ethnicity are important parts of American culture and society. It ignores reality to pretend otherwise. People make all sorts of judgments based upon them. A parent should prepare his or her child for the realities of the world, including the prospect of racial discrimination. A parent who shares a particular race or ethnicity with his or her child may be best able to help the child deal with many self-identity and self-esteem issues related to those subjects.

The United States Supreme Court has prohibited the use of race as the sole factor in custody decisions, though it did not rule that race could not be one factor among many. Lower courts have confirmed that race is a permissible factor, as long as it is not the sole factor in the custody decision. This is a sensible legal position, considering the hurdles biracial children may need to overcome in an American society with more subtle forms of racial discrimination. Moreover, racial identity is an important part of any child's development. A parent who shares racial and cultural characteristics with a child often may be in the best position to assist the child in key developmental and emotional issues that arise during life. Considering the race of the parent vis-à-vis the child is more often than not in the best interests of the child.

The Future
of Child Custody

C hild custody disputes are likely to continue, given the high
level of divorce in the United States. A major source of controversy in child custody cases stems from situations in which
a parent takes the children to another jurisdiction beyond the
apparent reach of U.S. laws. Consider for example the plight
of Christopher Savoie, a Tennessee-based man whose former
wife took the couple's two children and left the country for her
native Japan. Savoie traveled to Japan to try to retrieve his young
son and daughter but ended up in a Japanese jail for a few days
before being released.[1]

The Savoie incident and others caused Representative
Christopher Smith to introduce and renew calls for passage of
his bill called the International Child Abduction Prevention
Act of 2009, which would "ensure compliance with the 1980
Hague Convention on the Civil Aspects of International Child

Abduction by countries with which the United States enjoys reciprocal obligations, to establish procedures for the prompt return of children abducted to other countries, and for other purposes."[2] "Our current system is not providing justice for left behind parents or for children whisked away from their mom and dad," said Smith. "Congress must act so that more children are not further traumatized by parental abduction."[3]

Religious Divisions and Mediation Techniques

Another continuing source of controversy is the role of religion in child custody cases. At one time, it was rarer for people

International Child Abduction Prevention Act of 2009

Representative Christopher Smith of New Jersey introduced this bill into Congress at the time of the Savoie incident. Though the bill was referred to committee, it did not become law. The following is an excerpt:

(b) Sense of Congress—It is the sense of Congress that the United States should set a strong example for other Hague Convention countries in the timely location and return of children wrongly removed from and retained in the United States.

(c) Purposes—The purposes of this Act are to—

(1) protect United States children from the harmful effects of international child abduction and to protect the right of children to exercise parental access with their parents in a safe and predictable way, wherever located;

(2) provide parents, their advocates, and judges the information they need to enhance the resolution of family disputes through established legal procedures, the tools for assessing the risk of wrongful removal and retention of children, and the practical means for overcoming obstacles to recovering abducted children;

of different faiths to intermarry. Today, however, parents who subscribe to different religious beliefs often argue about which religion a child will be exposed to and will practice, both during a marriage and in custody proceedings. The parents might disagree about whether the child should be raised Catholic or Baptist, Christian or Jewish, or Buddhist or Muslim. Regardless of the religious preference, what is clear is that there has been a marked increase in the number of religious disputes in child custody cases.[4]

Judges, however, have to be careful when delving into the religious practices of parents. The Free Exercise Clause of the

(3) establish effective mechanisms to provide assistance to and aggressive advocacy on behalf of parents whose children have been abducted from the United States to a foreign country, from a foreign country to the United States, and on behalf of military parents stationed abroad;

(4) promote an international consensus that the best interests of children are of paramount importance in matters relating to their custody, and that it is in the best interest of a child to have issues of custody determined in the State of their habitual residence immediately prior to the abduction;

(5) provide the necessary training for military officials and training and assistance to military families to address the unique circumstances of the resolution of child custody disputes which occur abroad, or occur when a parent is serving abroad;

(6) facilitate the creation and effective implementation of international mechanisms, particularly the 1980 Hague Convention on the Civil Aspects of International Child Abduction, to protect children from the harmful effects of their wrongful removal and retention; and

(7) facilitate the compliance of the United States with reciprocal obligations contained in the Hague Convention regarding children wrongfully removed to or retained in the United States.

Source: H.R. 3240.

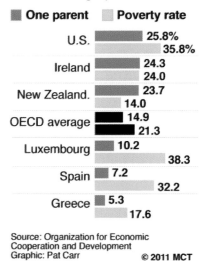

Single parents

Among industrialized countries, the U.S. has the highest percentage of single-parent families and more than a third of them live in poverty. OECD countries with the highest and lowest single-parent rates:

■ One parent   Poverty rate

	One parent	Poverty rate
U.S.	25.8%	35.8%
Ireland	24.3	24.0
New Zealand.	23.7	14.0
OECD average	14.9	21.3
Luxembourg	10.2	38.3
Spain	7.2	32.2
Greece	5.3	17.6

Source: Organization for Economic
Cooperation and Development
Graphic: Pat Carr   © 2011 MCT

This 2011 chart shows countries in the Organization for Econcomic Cooperation and Development (OECD) with the highest and lowest percentage of households with single parents and the poverty rate among them. The United States has the highest percentage of one-parent families, more than one-third of whom live in poverty.

First Amendment provides individuals with protection from governmental intrusions into their religious liberty rights. Legal scholar and family law attorney Joanne Ross Wilder writes that it is important for courts to "recognize the parental rights" in child custody cases "and accord appropriate deference to those rights."[5] Courts will have to grapple carefully with the issue of religion as it arises in more and more custody cases.

Another emerging issue concerns the use of mediation techniques to resolve more family law disputes. More social science literature establishes that high-conflict family litigation, especially including protracted custody disputes, has a negative impact on children. Some states, such as Florida, have turned to alternative dispute resolution techniques to attempt to mitigate these problems. Florida allows for the appointment of a "parent coordinator" to aid in reducing the conflict between the parties.[6]

Children of Homosexual Couples

Finally, another critical issue to consider is the status of children in custody disputes between same-sex couples. In 1996, the U.S. Congress passed the Defense of Marriage Act (DOMA), which was signed into law by President Bill Clinton. In addition to defining marriage as being between one man and one woman, the law also provided that no state or territory of the United States be required to recognize a same-sex relationship as marriage that may have been considered a marriage in another state. As of August 2011, 40 out of 50 states prohibit same-sex marriage, either through their individual state constitutions or statutes.

As most states in the United States do not recognize same-sex marriages or unions, complications often arise when a parent who has lived in a state that allows same-sex unions leaves his or her partner and moves to a state that does not recognize same-sex marriages or custody arrangements. Will a state in which same-sex marriages are prohibited recognize child support, visitation rights, or other custody issues that may arise? As the nation grapples with developing uniform standards for child custody issues in general, the adopted or biological children of homosexual couples provide a new challenge to the U.S. legal system.

(continues on page 82)

Excerpt from the Florida Law on Parent Coordinators

§ 61.125. Parenting coordination

(1) *Purpose.*—The purpose of parenting coordination is to provide a child-focused alternative dispute resolution process whereby a parenting coordinator assists the parents in creating or implementing a parenting plan by facilitating the resolution of disputes between the parents by providing education, making recommendations, and, with the prior approval of the parents and the court, making limited decisions within the scope of the court's order of referral.

(2) *Referral.*—In any action in which a judgment or order has been sought or entered adopting, establishing, or modifying a parenting plan, except for a domestic violence proceeding under chapter 741, and upon agreement of the parties, the court's own motion, or the motion of a party, the court may appoint a parenting coordinator and refer the parties to parenting coordination to assist in the resolution of disputes concerning their parenting plan.

(3) *Domestic violence issues.*

    (a) If there has been a history of domestic violence, the court may not refer the parties to parenting coordination unless both parents consent. The court shall offer each party an opportunity to consult with an attorney or domestic violence advocate before accepting the party's consent. The court must determine whether each party's consent has been given freely and voluntarily. . . .

    (c) If there is a history of domestic violence, the court shall order safeguards to protect the safety of the participants, including, but not limited to, adherence to all provisions of an injunction for protection or conditions of bail, probation, or a sentence arising from criminal proceedings.

(4) *Qualifications of a parenting coordinator.*—A parenting coordinator is an impartial third person whose role is to assist the parents in successfully creating or implementing a parenting plan. Unless there is a written agreement between the parties, the court may appoint only a qualified parenting coordinator.

(a) To be qualified, a parenting coordinator must:

    1. Meet one of the following professional requirements:

        a. Be licensed as a mental health professional under chapter 490 or chapter 491.

        b. Be licensed as a physician under chapter 458, with certification by the American Board of Psychiatry and Neurology

        c. Be certified by the Florida Supreme Court as a family law mediator, with at least a master's degree in a mental health field.

        d. Be a member in good standing of The Florida Bar.

    2. Complete all of the following:

        a. Three years of postlicensure or postcertification practice.

        b. A family mediation training program certified by the Florida Supreme Court.

        c. A minimum of 24 hours of parenting coordination training in parenting coordination concepts and ethics, family systems theory and application, family dynamics in separation and divorce, child and adolescent development, the parenting coordination process, parenting coordination techniques, and Florida family law and procedure, and a minimum of 4 hours of training in domestic violence and child abuse which is related to parenting coordination.

(b) The court may require additional qualifications to address issues specific to the parties.

(c) A qualified parenting coordinator must be in good standing, or in clear and active status, with his or her respective licensing authority, certification board, or both, as applicable.

(5) *Disqualifications of parenting coordinator.*

    (a) The court may not appoint a person to serve as parenting coordinator who, in any jurisdiction:

(continues)

(continued)

1. Has been convicted or had adjudication withheld on a charge of child abuse, child neglect, domestic violence, parental kidnapping, or interference with custody;

2. Has been found by a court in a child protection hearing to have abused, neglected, or abandoned a child;

3. Has consented to an adjudication or a withholding of adjudication on a petition for dependency; or

4. Is or has been a respondent in a final order or injunction of protection against domestic violence.

(b) A parenting coordinator must discontinue service as a parenting coordinator and immediately report to the court and the parties if any of the disqualifying circumstances described in paragraph (a) occur, or if he or she no longer meets the minimum qualifications in subsection (4), and the court may appoint another parenting coordinator. . . .

(7) *Confidentiality.*—Except as otherwise provided in this section, all communications made by, between, or among the parties and the parenting coordinator during parenting coordination sessions are confidential. The parenting coordinator and each party designated in the order appointing the coordinator may not testify or offer evidence about communications made by, between, or among the parties and the parenting coordinator during parenting coordination sessions, except if:

(a) Necessary to identify, authenticate, confirm, or deny a written agreement entered into by the parties during parenting coordination;

(continued from page 79)

Summary

The United States has the highest divorce rate in the world. For that reason, child custody disputes will continue to occur. States must continue to work on developing a standard set of factors

(b) The testimony or evidence is necessary to identify an issue for resolution by the court without otherwise disclosing communications made by any party or the parenting coordinator;

(c) The testimony or evidence is limited to the subject of a party's compliance with the order of referral to parenting coordination, orders for psychological evaluation, counseling ordered by the court or recommended by a health care provider, or for substance abuse testing or treatment;

(d) The parenting coordinator reports that the case is no longer appropriate for parenting coordination;

(e) The parenting coordinator is reporting that he or she is unable or unwilling to continue to serve and that a successor parenting coordinator should be appointed;

(f) The testimony or evidence is necessary pursuant to paragraph (5)(b) or subsection (8);

(g) The parenting coordinator is not qualified to address or resolve certain issues in the case and a more qualified coordinator should be appointed;

(h) The parties agree that the testimony or evidence be permitted; or

(i) The testimony or evidence is necessary to protect any person from future acts that would constitute domestic violence under chapter 741; child abuse, neglect, or abandonment under chapter 39; or abuse, neglect, or exploitation of an elderly or disabled adult under chapter 825....

Source: Fla. Stat. § 61.125.

that truly will address the best interests of children involved in custody disputes and refine a system that will likely see ever more custodial parents seeking to relocate in this global economy. Whatever the mitigating circumstances—race, religion, ethnicity, sexual orientation—the needs of the children are paramount.

With effort and an eye on securing children's best interests, the legal system will continue to develop a more equitable system to manage these cases. Society must do all that it can to ensure that children are protected as well as possible. Our nation's future— our children—depend on it.

Beginning Legal Research

The goals of each book in the Point/Counterpoint series are not only to give the reader a basic introduction to a controversial issue affecting society, but also to encourage the reader to explore the issue more fully. This Appendix is meant to serve as a guide to the reader in researching the current state of the law as well as exploring some of the public policy arguments as to why existing laws should be changed or new laws are needed.

Although some sources of law can be found primarily in law libraries, legal research has become much faster and more accessible with the advent of the Internet. This Appendix discusses some of the best starting points for free access to laws and court decisions, but surfing the Web will uncover endless additional sources of information. Before you can research the law, however, you must have a basic understanding of the American legal system.

The most important source of law in the United States is the Constitution. Originally enacted in 1787, the Constitution outlines the structure of our federal government, as well as setting limits on the types of laws that the federal government and state governments can enact. Through the centuries, a number of amendments have added to or changed the Constitution, most notably the first 10 amendments, which collectively are known as the "Bill of Rights" and which guarantee important civil liberties.

Reading the plain text of the Constitution provides little information. For example, the Constitution prohibits "unreasonable searches and seizures" by the police. To understand concepts in the Constitution, it is necessary to look to the decisions of the U.S. Supreme Court, which has the ultimate authority in interpreting the meaning of the Constitution. For example, the U.S. Supreme Court's 2001 decision in *Kyllo v. United States* held that scanning the outside of a person's house using a heat sensor to determine whether the person is growing marijuana is an unreasonable search—if it is done without first getting a search warrant from a judge. Each state also has its own constitution and a supreme court that is the ultimate authority on its meaning.

Also important are the written laws, or "statutes," passed by the U.S. Congress and the individual state legislatures. As with constitutional provisions, the U.S. Supreme Court and the state supreme courts are the ultimate authorities in interpreting the meaning of federal and state laws, respectively. However, the U.S. Supreme Court might find that a state law violates the U.S. Constitution, and a state supreme court might find that a state law violates either the state or U.S. Constitution.

Not every controversy reaches either the U.S. Supreme Court or the state supreme courts, however. Therefore, the decisions of other courts are also important. Trial courts hear evidence from both sides and make a decision, while appeals courts review the decisions made by trial courts. Sometimes rulings from appeals courts are appealed further to the U.S. Supreme Court or the state supreme courts.

Lawyers and courts refer to statutes and court decisions through a formal system of citations. Use of these citations reveals which court made the decision or which legislature passed the statute, and allows one to quickly locate the statute or court case online or in a law library. For example, the Supreme Court case *Brown v. Board of Education* has the legal citation 347 U.S. 483 (1954). At a law library, this 1954 decision can be found on page 483 of volume 347 of the U.S. Reports, which are the official collection of the Supreme Court's decisions. On the following page, you will find samples of all the major kinds of legal citation.

Finding sources of legal information on the Internet is relatively simple thanks to "portal" sites such as findlaw.com and lexisone.com, which allow the user to access a variety of constitutions, statutes, court opinions, law review articles, news articles, and other useful sources of information. For example, findlaw.com offers access to all Supreme Court decisions since 1893. Other useful sources of information include gpo.gov, which contains a complete copy of the U.S. Code, and thomas.loc.gov, which offers access to bills pending before Congress, as well as recently passed laws. Of course, the Internet changes every second of every day, so it is best to do some independent searching.

Of course, many people still do their research at law libraries, some of which are open to the public. For example, some state governments and universities offer the public access to their law collections. Law librarians can be of great assistance, as even experienced attorneys need help with legal research from time to time.

Common Citation Forms

Source of Law	Sample Citation	Notes
U.S. Supreme Court	*Employment Division v. Smith*, 485 U.S. 660 (1988)	The U.S. Reports is the official record of Supreme Court decisions. There is also an unofficial Supreme Court ("S. Ct.") reporter.
U.S. Court of Appeals	*United States v. Lambert*, 695 F.2d 536 (11th Cir.1983)	Appellate cases appear in the Federal Reporter, designated by "F." The 11th Circuit has jurisdiction in Alabama, Florida, and Georgia.
U.S. District Court	*Carillon Importers, Ltd. v. Frank Pesce Group, Inc.*, 913 F.Supp. 1559 (S.D.Fla.1996)	Federal trial-level decisions are reported in the Federal Supplement ("F. Supp."). Some states have multiple federal districts; this case originated in the Southern District of Florida.
U.S. Code	Thomas Jefferson Commemoration Commission Act, 36 U.S.C., §149 (2002)	Sometimes the popular names of legislation—names with which the public may be familiar—are included with the U.S. Code citation.
State Supreme Court	*Sterling v. Cupp*, 290 Ore. 611, 614, 625 P.2d 123, 126 (1981)	The Oregon Supreme Court decision is reported in both the state's reporter and the Pacific regional reporter.
State Statute	Pennsylvania Abortion Control Act of 1982, 18 Pa. Cons. Stat. 3203-3220 (1990)	States use many different citation formats for their statutes.

Cases

Farmer v. Farmer, 439 N.Y.S.2d 584 (N.Y. 1981)

In this decision, the New York court ruled that race could not be a factor in a child custody dispute between parents of different races.

Palmore v. Sidoti, 466 U.S. 429 (1984)

In this decision, the U.S. Supreme Court ruled that race cannot be the primary factor in a child custody determination. The Court ruled that a trial judge violated the Equal Protection Clause of the Fourteenth Amendment when he allowed a father to obtain custody of his child simply because his former wife entered into an interracial marriage. The case stands for the principle that race cannot be the sole or main factor in a child custody proceeding.

Jones v. Jones, 542 N.W.2d 119 (S.D. 1996)

In this decision, the South Dakota Supreme Court ruled that a lower court could consider the fact that a Native American father might be able to better assist his biracial child with certain issues because of his ethnicity. The court ruled that race or ethnicity could be one of many factors in a custody determination.

Cranston v. Combs, 106 S.W.3d 641 (Tenn. 2003)

In this decision, the Tennessee Supreme Court ruled that a parent could not obtain a change in custody unless he or she could show a material change in circumstances that would justify such a measure.

Toler v. Toler, 947 So.2d 416 (Ala.Civ.App. 2006)

In this decision, an Alabama appeals court changed custody from a mother to the father, finding that the mother's relocation of the children was not in the best interests of the children.

In Re Marriage of Gambla, 853 N.E.2d 847 (Ill.App. 2006)

In this decision, an Illinois appeals court ruled that a trial judge did not err in considering race as one of many factors in awarding custody of a biracial child to her African-American mother rather than her Caucasian father. The appeals court said that the mother may be able to help the child better cope with racial identity issues and said that race could be one of many factors in a child custody proceeding.

Gilbert v. Gilbert, 730 N.W.2d 833 (N.D. 2007)

In this decision, the North Dakota Supreme Court ruled that the presumption should be placed in favor of the primary custodial parent when he or she engages in a relocation of the child. Unless the other parent can show bad motive or ill will, the relocation will be presumed valid and approved.

Terms and Concepts

Best interests of the child
Child custody
Domestic violence

Equal Protection Clause
Joint custody
Material change in circumstances
Noncustodial parent
Primary custodial parent
Shared custody
Sole custody
Tender Years Doctrine
Virtual visitation

Introduction: An Overview of Child Custody

1 Susan W. Savard, "Through the Eyes of a Child: Impact and Measures to Protect Children in High-Conflict Family Law Litigation," 84 *Florida Bar Journal* 57 (2010).
2 David L. Hudson Jr. *The Handy Law Answer Book.* Visible Ink Press, 2010, pp. 294–295.
3 Cal. Fam. Code § 3003.
4 Cal. Fam. Code § 3004.
5 Cal. Fam. Code § 3006.
6 Cal. Fam. Code § 3007.
7 *Cranston v. Combs*, 106 S.W.3d 641 (Tenn. 2003).

Point: The Best Interests Standard Works in Child Custody Disputes

1 Steven N. Peskind, "Determining the Undeterminable: The Best Interest of the Child Standard as an Imperfect but Necessary Guidepost to Determine Child Custody," 25 *Northern Illinois University Law Review* 449, 451 (2005).
2 Peskind at p. 454.
3 *Grubbs v. Grubbs*, 623 P.2d 546, 548–549 (Kan. 1981).
4 *Bah v. Bah*, 668 S.W.2d 663, 666 (Tenn. App. 1983).
5 Shannon Dean Sexton, "Custody System Free of Gender Preferences and Consistent with the Best Interests of the Child: Suggestions for a More Protective and Equitable Custody System," 88 *Kentucky Law Journal* 761, 769–770 (2000).
6 New York Court Help, "Child Custody & Visitation," http://www.courts.state.ny.us/courthelp/faqs/childcustody.html.
7 Ibid.
8 Ind. Code Ann. § 31-14-13-2 (7).
9 MCLS § 722.23(i).
10 Peskind at p. 457.
11 Lynne Marie Kohm, "Tracing the Foundations of the Best Interests of the Child Standard in American Jurisprudence," 10 *Journal of Law & Family Studies* 337, 337 (2008).
12 Steven N. Peskind, "Determining the Undeterminable: The Best Interest of the Child Standard as an Imperfect but Necessary Guidepost to Determine

Child Custody," 25 *Northern Illinois University Law Review* 449, 451 (2005).
13 Ibid.

Counterpoint: The Best Interests Standard Is Too Subjective

1 Burns Ind. Code Ann. § 31-14-13-2(1).
2 ORS § 107.137(1)(e).
3 Va. Code Ann. § 20-124.3.
4 13 Del.C § 722(8)("The criminal history of any party or any other resident of the household including whether the criminal history contains pleas of guilty or no contest or a conviction of a criminal offense.").
5 A.R.S. § 25-403 (A)(10).
6 Mont. Code Anno., § 40-4-212 (j) and (k).
7 O.C.G.A. 19-9-3(K).
8 Minn. Stat. § 257C.04 (11).
9 Nev. Rev. Stat. Ann. § 125.480(i).
10 Idaho Code § 2-717(1)(e).
11 C.R.S. 14-10-124(a)(XI).
12 John De Witt Gregory, Peter N. Swisher, and Sheryl L. Wolf. *Understanding Family Law* (3d). Lexis-Nexis: Newark, N.J., 2005, p. 441.
13 Lynne Marie Kohm, "Tracing the Foundations of the Best Interests of the Child Standard in American Jurisprudence," 10 *Journal of Law & Family Studies* 337, 339 (2008).
14 O.C.G.A. 19-9-1(3).

Point: Laws Should Favor the Custodial Parent in Relocation Disputes

1 *Latimer v. Farmer*, 602 S.E.2d 32, 34 (S.C. 2004).
2 *Kaiser v. Kaiser*, 23 P.3d 278, 284 (Ok. 2001).
3 Janet Leigh Richards, "Children's Rights v. Parent's Rights: A Proposed Solution to the Custodial Relocation Conundrum," 29 *New Mexico Law Review* 245, 260 (1999).
4 Robert L. Gottsfield, "Relocating Andy: Remaining with the Nurturer as Guiding Principle: Impact of Relocation Statute: How to Win a Removal Case," 36 *Arizona Attorney* 10, 10 (2000).
5 Ibid.
6 T.C.A. § 36-6-108.

7 *Latimer v. Farmer*, 602 S.E.2d at 34.

8 *Gilbert v. Gilbert*, 730 N.W.2d 833, 838 (N.D. 2007).

9 Cal. Fam. Code § 7501.

10 S.D. Codified Laws § 25-5-13.

11 *Kaiser v. Kaiser*, 23 P.3d at 282.

12 Anne LeVasseur, "Virtual Visitation: How Will Courts Respond to a New and Emerging Issue?" 17 *Quinnipiac Probate Law Journal* 362 (2004); Samara Nazir, "The Changing Path to Relocation: An Update on Post-Divorce Relocation Issues," 22 *Journal of American Academy of Matrimonial Lawyers* 483 (2009).

Counterpoint: The Interests of the Noncustodial Parent Should Be Given Greater Protection

1 *Levine v. Levine*, 705 A.2d 1204 (N.J. 1998).

2 Proctor Harang, "Custody and Visitation: The Relocation Controversy," 16 *Journal of Contemporary Legal Issues* 255, 259 (2007).

3 IC 31-17-2.2-5(c).

4 Ala.Code 1975 § 30-3-169.4.

5 *Toler v. Toler*, 947 So.2d 416, 422 (Ala. Civ.App. 2006).

6 Ibid.

7 Elisabeth Bach-Van Horn, "Virtual Visitation: Are Webcams Being Used as an Excuse to Allow Relocation?" 21 *Journal of the American Academy of Matrimonial Lawyers* 171, 189 (2008).

8 William G. Austin, "Relocation, Research, and Forensic Evaluation, Part I: Effects of Residential Mobility on Children of Divorce," 46 *Family Court Review* 137, 137 (2008).

9 Austin at p. 141.

10 Ibid. at 144.

11 Elisabeth Bach-Van Horn, "Virtual Visitation: Are Webcams Being Used as an Excuse to Allow Relocation?" 21 *Journal of the American Academy of Matrimonial Lawyers* 171, 172 (2008).

12 F.S.A. § 61.13003(b)(4).

13 N.C.G.S.A. § 50-13.2(e).

Point: Race Should Not Be a Factor in Child Custody Decisions

1 *Palmore v. Sidoti*, 466 U.S. 429 (1984).

2 Ibid. at 431.

3 Ibid.

4 Ibid. at 432.

5 Ibid. at 434.

6 *Farmer v. Farmer*, 439 N.Y.S.2d 584 (N.Y. 1981).

7 Ibid. at 586.

8 Ibid. at 589.

9 *Tipton v. Aaron*, 185 S.W.3d 142 (Ark. App. 2004).

10 Ibid. at 148.

11 Ibid.

12 Ibid. at 150.

13 *In Re Marriage of Gambla*, 853 N.E.2d 847, 968 (Ill.App. 2006).

14 Ibid. at 876 (J. McLaren, dissenting).

15 Wis. Stat. 767.24(5).

16 D.C. Code Ann. § 16-914.

17 Minn. Stat. Ann. § 260C.193, Subd. 3.

18 42 U.S.C. § 622.

19 § 453.005 R.S.Mo.

20 David D. Meyer, "Palmore Comes of Age: The Place of Race in the Placement of Children," 18 *University of Florida Journal of Law & Policy* 183, 202 (2007).

21 Ibid. at 206.

Counterpoint: Race Is a Valid Concern in Child Custody Disputes

1 Gayle Pollock, "The Role of Race in Child Custody Decisions Between Natural Parents Over Biracial Children," 23 *New York University School of Law Review of Law and Social Change*, 603, 605 (1997).

2 *Palmore v. Sidoti*, 466 U.S. 429, 432 (1984).

3 *Palmore v. Sidoti*, 466 U.S. 429, 434 (1984).

4 *In Re Marriage of Gambla*, 853 N.E.2d 847 (Ill.App. 2006).

5 *In Re Marriage of Gambla*, 853 N.E.2d at 869.

6 *Ebirim v. Ebirim*, 620 N.W.2d 117, 121 (Neb.App. 2000).

7 M.S.A. § 518.17(11).

8 *Jones v. Jones*, 542 N.W.2d 119, 123–124 (S.D. 1996).

9 *Jones v. Jones*, 542 N.W.2d 119, 123 (S.D. 1996).

10 *In Re Marriage of Gambla*, 853 N.E.2d at 858.

11 *In Re Marriage of Gambla*, 853 N.E.2d at 868.

12 Evan B. Donaldson Adoption Institute, "Finding Families for African American Children: The Role of Race & Law in Adoption Practice," May 2008, p. 44, http://www.adoptioninstitute.org/publications/MEPApaper20080527.pdf.

13 Ibid. at 25.

Conclusion: The Future of Child Custody

1 "American jailed in Japan for trying to reclaim his children," CNN.com, September 29, 2009.

2 H.R. 2340 (introduced 7/26/2009).

3 Erin Duffy, "Smith renews call for child-abduction act," *The Times of Trenton*, October 1, 2009, p. A04.

4 Neela Banerjee, "Religion Joins Custody Cases, to Judges' Unease," *New York Times*, February 13, 2008, http://www.nytimes.com/2008/02/13/us/13custody.html.

5 Joanne Ross Wilder, "Resolving Religious Disputes in Custody Cases: It's Really Not About Best Interests," 22 *Journal of American Academy of Matrimonial Lawyers* 411, 422 (2009).

6 Susan W. Savard, "Through the Eyes of a Child: Impact and Measures to Protect Children in High-Conflict Family Law Litigation," 84 *Florida Bar Journal* 57 (2010).

Books and Articles

Austin, William G. "Relocation, Research, and Forensic Evaluation, Part I: Effects of Residential Mobility on Children of Divorce," 46 *Family Court Review* 137 (2008).

Bach-Van Horn, Elisabeth. "Virtual Visitation: Are Webcams Being Used as an Excuse to Allow Relocation?" 21 *Journal of the American Academy of Matrimony Lawyers* 171, 189 (2008).

Breen, Claire. *The Standard of the Best Interests of the Child: A Western Tradition in International and Comparative Law*, 2002.

Crippen, Gary. "Stumbling Beyond the Best Interests of the Child: Reexamining Child Custody Standard-Setting in the Wake of Minnesota's Four Year Experiment with the Primary Caretaker Preference," 75 *Minnesota Law Review* 427 (1990).

Elster, Jon. "Solomonic Judgments: Against the Best Interests of the Child," 54 *University of Chicago Law Review* 1 (1987).

Evan B. Donaldson Adoption Institute. "Finding Families for African American Children: The Role of Race & Law in Adoption Practice," May 2008, http://www.adoptioninstitute.org/publications/MEPApaper20080527.pdf.

Gottsfield, Robert L. "Relocating Andy: Remaining with the Nurturer as Guiding Principle: Impact of Relocation Statute: How to Win a Removal Case," 36 *Arizona Attorney* 10 (2000).

Gregory, John De Witt, Peter N. Swisher, and Sheryl L. Wolf. *Understanding Family Law* (3d). Lexis-Nexis: Newark, N.J., 2005.

Harang, Proctor. "Custody and Visitation: The Relocation Controversy," 16 *Journal of Contemporary Legal Issues* 255 (2007).

Hudson, David L. Jr. *The Handy Law Answer Book*. Visible Ink Press: Detroit, Mich., 2010.

Jellum, Linda. "Parents Know Best: Revising Our Approach to Parental Custody Arrangements," 65 *Ohio State Law Journal* 615 (2004).

Kohm, Lynne Marie. "Tracing the Foundations of the Best Interests of the Child Standard in American Jurisprudence," 10 *Journal of Law & Family Studies* 337 (2008).

LeVasseur, Anne. "Virtual Visitation: How Will Courts Respond to a New and Emerging Issue?" 17 *Quinnipiac Probate Law Journal* 362 (2004).

Mercer, Kathyrn L. "A Content Analysis of Judicial Decision-Making: How Judges Use the Primary Caretaker Standard to Make a Custody Determination, 5 *William & Mary Journal of Women and the Law* 1 (1998).

Meyer, David D. "Palmore Comes of Age: The Place of Race in the Placement of Children," 18 *University of Florida Journal of Law & Policy* 183 (2007).

Nazir, Samara. "The Changing Path to Relocation: An Update on Post-Divorce Relocation Issues," 22 *Journal of American Academy of Matrimonial Lawyers* 483 (2009).

Peskind, Steven N. "Determining the Undeterminable: The Best Interest of the Child Standard as an Imperfect but Necessary Guidepost to Determine Child Custody," 25 *Northern Illinois University Law Review* 449 (2005).

Pollock, Gayle. "The Role of Race in Child Custody Decisions Between Natural Parents Over Biracial Children," 23 *New York University School of Law Review of Law and Social Change*, 603 (1997).

Richards, Janet Leigh. "Children's Rights v. Parent's Rights: A Proposed Solution to the Custodial Relocation Conundrum," 29 *New Mexico Law Review* 245 (1999).

Savard, Susan W. "Through the Eyes of a Child: Impact and Measures to Protect Children in High-Conflict Family Law Litigation," 84 *Florida Bar Journal* 57 (2010).

Schneider, Carl E. "On the Duties and Rights of Parents," 81 *Virginia Law Review* 2477 (1995).

Sexton, Shannon Dean. "Custody System Free of Gender Preferences and Consistent with the Best Interests of the Child: Suggestions for a More Protective and Equitable Custody System," 88 *Kentucky Law Journal* 761 (2000).

Wilder, Joanne Ross. "Religion and Best Interests in Custody Cases," 18 *Journal of American Academy of Matrimonial Lawyers* 211 (2002).

———. "Resolving Religious Disputes in Custody Cases: It's Really Not About Best Interests," 22 *Journal of American Academy of Matrimonial Lawyers* 411 (2009).

Woodhouse, Barbara Bennett. "Child Custody in the Age of Children's Rights: The Search for a Just and Workable Standard," 33 *Family Law Quarterly* 815 (1999).

Web Sites

Child Custody Organization
http://www.childcustody.org/
According to its Web site, "This organization is dedicated to providing you with the information you need to be successful in your endeavors to win or defend custody of your child."

Children's Rights Council
http://www.crckids.org/
Founded in 1985, this organization looks to raise awareness about the importance of keeping both parents in a child's life. It seeks to reduce or eliminate the difficulties a child faces growing up without both parents.

National Network on Family Law Policy
http://nnflp.blogspot.com/
According to its Web site, "The National Network on Family Law Policy (NNFLP), formed in 1999, is a privately-funded, nonpartisan, nonprofit association of professionals, scholars, and activist organizations in law, psychology, and sociology who provide support for amicus groups, and advocacy for appropriate reforms in family law legislation."

PICTURE CREDITS ▷

DAVID L. HUDSON JR. is a First Amendment Scholar at the First Amendment Center at Vanderbilt University. He teaches law classes at Middle Tennessee State University, Nashville School of Law, and Vanderbilt Law School. He is the author or coauthor of more than 30 books, including several in the POINT/COUNTERPOINT series.

He dedicates this book to three dedicated parents: Mike Rodgers, Tiffany Villager, and Angie McDade.

ALAN MARZILLI, M.A., J.D., lives in Washington, D.C., and is a senior writer for Advocates for Human Potential, Inc., a research and consulting firm based in Sudbury, Mass., and Albany, N.Y. He primarily works on developing training and educational materials for agencies of the federal government on topics such as housing, mental health policy, employment, and transportation. He has spoken on mental health issues in 30 states, the District of Columbia, and Puerto Rico; his work has included training mental health administrators, nonprofit management and staff, and people with mental illnesses and their families on a wide variety of topics, including effective advocacy, community-based mental health services, and housing. He has written several handbooks and training curricula that are used nationally and as far away as the territory of Guam. He managed statewide and national mental health advocacy programs and worked for several public interest lobbying organizations while studying law at Georgetown University. He has written more than a dozen books, including numerous titles in the POINT/COUNTERPOINT series.